MW01228197

Everything I Wish I Knew When I Was 18

Advice For Young Men to Create a Great Life for Themselves

Paul Bauer

ISBN: 9798867853402

Edited by Nick August and Nurse Chick
Audiobook Narrated by Paul Bauer and RP Thor
Book Cover by Paul Bauer

INTELLECTUAL PROPERTY

PROFESSIONAL DISCLAIMER

Although you may find the information, principles, applications, and general advice in this book useful, they are presented with the understanding that the author is not engaged in providing specific medical, psychological, emotional, spiritual, financial, legal, or sexual advice. Nor is anything in this book intended to be a diagnosis, prescription, recommendation, or cure for any specific kind of medical, psychological, emotional or sexual problem.

Each person has unique needs, and this book cannot take these individual differences into account. Each person should engage in a program of treatment, prevention, cure, and/or general health only in consultation with licensed, qualified, physicians, therapists, and/or other competent professionals.

ACKNOWLEDGEMENTS

Who hurt you? This is a question I often get on social media when I put out a video talking about the nature and psychology of women. My messages on social media aren't really meant to cast stones at women. They are there to shine a light on female nature so that men can better understand it, and so men can use the information to better navigate the sexual marketplace.

The fact of the matter is, that we've all been hurt by someone. Sometimes we've been hurt by multiple women. Smart men will use this pain as a learning experience so they can grow. That's exactly what I did.

With that being said, I would like to acknowledge the women who have hurt me in my life. You know who you are. There are two main ones, and I'm not going to name them here. They were the catalyst I needed for this journey, and for that, I am eternally grateful.

GIVE ME YOUR HONEST FEEDBACK

Thank you so much for buying my book! As a small indie publisher, it means a lot and I hope I am making a difference in your journey to level up.

If you have a moment, I would greatly appreciate your honest feedback on Amazon. Your review makes a huge difference for the book, and I'd love to know how the material has impacted you.

To leave your feedback:

1. Open your camera app
2. Point your mobile device at the QR code below and click the link that shows up
3. The review page will appear in your web browser

TABLE OF CONTENTS

INTRODUCTION

In the interests of full transparency, I wrote this introduction three times before completing this version. If anyone tells you that writing a book is easy, he is either lying or is a complete nerd. Writing is difficult, especially when you know that many people are going to read it and review it on Amazon. If you're reading this though, I finally found a formula for the book that worked for my literary style. You're welcome!

Let's be honest here: most people skip introductions, don't they? I could probably write anything here and it wouldn't even matter. In fact, I have a friend who wrote two books, and he said most people don't get past the cover. He pretty much uses his books as glorified business cards! I'm hoping that doesn't end up being the case for this book though. I really hope that you, the reader, get something out of this book.

You see, at the time of this writing, I am forty-two years old, and will probably be forty-three by the time I finally finish it and publish it. It took me this long to learn everything I'm about to talk about in the following pages. If a few of you readers absorb this material and start applying it at an early age, then I will consider this book a success! I really do wish that I learned all of this when I was eighteen. It would have made my life so much easier.

But alas, I did not. In fact, if you are a young person reading this, I'm willing to bet this material goes in one ear and out the other if you read any of this at all. I don't mean to insult you. It's just how things typically go with most young men. We tend to act as though we know everything at that age and don't listen to those who have gone before us. I was the same way, so I certainly can't blame you for doing the same. My dad used to say that our brains go dormant at thirteen years old, and you don't start coming out of it until around twenty-five. When your brain does wake up, you realize how smart your parents got over the last twelve years.

I'm guessing that people who read this entire book will probably be in their mid to late thirties, or even older. That's typically when a lot of us go searching for answers to things. A lot of that is because something happens in our lives to force our hands. It can be anything from divorce, to losing a job, to even a death in the family. There can be any number of reasons people go looking for answers. The important thing is that they take action to find the answers they are looking for!

So, what are you going to learn about in this book? When I was a kid, one of my most important mentors was my Karate Sensei, Fred Bode. He was monumental in my life for several reasons but mainly his philosophy on mindset. Mindset can make or break a person, and quite a bit of this book ultimately comes down to mindset. Mr. Bode taught us to always develop ourselves mentally, physically, and spiritually. All of that is going to be discussed in this book. What he didn't teach us, what I wish I knew more about at eighteen, was about love and relationships and how to make money and build wealth.

So, what follows will be an introduction to things from spirituality to education and career choice, and how to build riches so you can achieve what every man really wants: Freedom. I'll also talk about the importance of diet and fitness and how it applies to your health. Finally, we'll discuss what all young horny men want to know. How to get the girls!

Too many young men get these concepts backwards though. There is a clear linear path of importance that I am going to outline in this book, and I've purposefully put women last on this list. There is a reason for that. You see, the more focus you put on your purpose in life, the better-quality women you will attract. Too many guys focus on chasing tail instead of chasing excellence and end up in failing marriages with women they hate. I know. I was one of those guys. So, I'm hoping you can learn from my mistakes here, and that you end up with a life much easier and fulfilling than mine was at your age.

THE LAW OF ATTRACTION IS REAL

Chances are you've heard of The Law of Attraction before. It's a concept that has been around for thousands of years but only recently became popular with the release of the movie *The Secret* in 2006. At its core, the idea is that like attracts like, and there are at least three ways to explain how it works and why it works either from a spiritual perspective, a quantum science perspective, or from a psychological perspective.

Here's the thing though: people all have their biases. Maybe you belong to one type of religion, or you're a complete atheist. In that case, you might find the spiritual explanation hard to swallow, even though The Law of Attraction goes hand-in-hand with pretty much all religions according to my understanding of it. Because of that, I decided not to address it from a spiritual standpoint.

Understanding quantum theory can be challenging or at least complicated, so trying to explain it from that perspective might cause many to tune out this chapter completely, so I decided not to try to explain it from a quantum science perspective.

That really leaves the psychological explanation, which I think is the easiest to understand for most people. I decided that this was the best way to go after talking with several authors and authorities who clearly understood that it works but didn't really buy the other explanations themselves. This explanation is also the most accessible because most of us have a general understanding of psychological concepts.

In reality, The Law of Attraction just works, and it really doesn't matter why you believe it does. I've seen it work in my life so many times that I just can't deny it at this point. One of the best *no bullshit* books on the subject is *The Science of Getting Rich* by Wallace D. Wattles. It's a short read, but he breaks it down into a set of steps you can follow to achieve anything you want and gives very little explanation as to why it works. I'm going to at least try to offer an explanation.

Why should you care? Well, here's the thing: The Law of Attraction is always working whether you know it or not, or whether you believe it or not, so you might as well learn to use it to your advantage. It also puts the outcome of your life story in your own hands. It gives you the power to write your life story in the exact way you want it to turn out. This is why I made this the first chapter. If you can master this, then you can achieve everything else that follows in this book with ease.

The Law of Attraction can be broken down into the idea that *thoughts become things*. The house you live in today, the car you drive, and the town you live in were all started by someone's thoughts. Those thoughts were turned into reality based on someone's actions, right? That's another key concept I want you to remember: The Law of Attraction is nothing without action!

This is something that I think the movie **The Secret** didn't touch on well enough. They mentioned this most important principle almost in passing that when you get the intuition to act on something, you need to jump on it. This is one of the largest criticisms of that movie. The way they laid everything out made it seem like The Universe is a big genie just granting wishes, and magical thinking will get you everything you want in life. That's one of the reasons I opted to not go for the spiritual explanation of it because atheists and non-believers will chalk it all up to magical thinking, and magical thinking is not what is at work here.

The movie **The Secret** also breaks down how The Law of Attraction works into three easy steps:

- Ask
- Believe
- Receive

That's kind of how it works, but those steps are extremely oversimplified.

So how does it work from a psychological perspective? Essentially, we get what we tend to focus on in life from a subconscious perspective. That's why I say that it's always working whether you believe in it or not, or if you're aware of it or not. The problem with not being aware of it is that most of us tend to focus on what we DON'T want, or what we DON'T have. We tend to focus on scarcity as opposed to abundance. That's also why a lot of people don't think The Law of Attraction works.

So, let's break down the three easy steps above and mold them into how it works in our minds, starting with **Ask.** You're supposed to ask The Universe for what you actually want. Maybe it's a better job, a better romantic partner, or a new car. It can literally be anything. From your brain's standpoint, you're essentially setting a goal. The best part about setting this goal is that you don't need to know how you will achieve this goal. You just need to focus on the goal itself and believe you already have it, and our miraculous subconscious mind will work night and day to figure out how to make it a reality.

The key here is believing you already have it, and that's the tricky part. **Believe** is also the second part in the list. The problem most people have with this step is that they want a particular goal to come to fruition, but their subconscious doesn't believe it's possible. Think of someone who grew up in a housing project and lived off ramen and canned tuna most of his life. His experience is only poverty, so believing that he can obtain a million dollars is difficult for him to grasp. Because of this, there will always be some doubt in his subconscious mind that he will be unable to achieve this goal, and that doubt will prevent him from achieving it. I'll explain in a bit how to fix this belief.

The last step is **Receive**, and this is another problem for many people. They want a million dollars or a fancy car, but they're not ready to receive one. What do I mean by *not ready*? Let's use the car as an example, and let's say you have a two-car garage. Both bays are occupied by your two broken down cars, or maybe one side has a car in it, and the other side is full of storage items. Whatever, it doesn't matter. The point is that you don't have room in your life for the new car. You're not ready to receive it. The spiritual folks will say that you are sending a message to the Universe that you're not ready to receive it. That you don't have space in your life to receive it. In reality, your subconscious tells you that you're not ready, so you need to make some room in your life for the things you want.

Another thing that happens is that you don't have the right mindset to have and keep the things you want. Did you know that most people who win the lottery end up broke in just a few years? It's because they don't have the mindset of a wealthy person. They weren't ready to receive that money, so it left them shortly after they received it. If you want millions of dollars, you need to start thinking like a wealthy person. Study their behavior. Learn what rich people do. Only then will you be ready to receive the wealth you have set your mind on. The funny thing about this is that by studying what rich people do, you will learn how rich people get rich, and you will probably figure out how to get that money you set as your goal. Are you beginning to see how this stuff works now?

So, let's get back to **Believe** because that is the core concept of this. How do you convince your subconscious to believe something that you truly don't believe? Have you ever heard the expression that if you tell a lie long enough, you start to believe it? It's because repeating that lie essentially programs your subconscious into believing it's true. It's the repetition of the lie that you repeat over and over that eventually seeps into your subconscious.

We can do the same thing with *autosuggestion*, also called *affirmations*. Like I said before, you must convince your subconscious that you already have the thing or things you want. You do that by writing out the things you want in the present tense. For example, if you want a new Toyota Tundra TRD Pro edition truck, you will write out on a piece of paper:

I'm grateful for my new Toyota Tundra TRD Pro truck!

I like to write these out on the back of a business card and laminate it so that I can keep my goals in my pocket. I'll explain why here in a minute.

Next, you want to look at that piece of paper or business card and read out loud what you wrote five times in the morning when you first wake up, and again five times in the evening just before going to bed. You do this because when you first wake up, you're still partially in your sleep state where your subconscious is most susceptible to suggestion. You also want to do this before bedtime because when you fall asleep, your subconscious stays working all night solving problems, and you want it to start solving the problem on how to make what you want a reality. Doing this before bed gets that ball rolling.

Another thing you want to do to convince your subconscious that you already have accomplished your goals, is to mentally visualize having already attained that goal, and that includes trying to feel what it would be like to have achieved it. Consider the truck as an example. You will think about how great it is to drive it. Imagine what the leather seats feel like. Imagine what the engine sounds like when you drive it down the highway. This will reinforce your subconscious because it has a hard time distinguishing what is real between your imagination and real life. Do this as you are reading your goal out loud in the morning and evening.

Naturally, you probably have a few goals you want to achieve. A great way to list out your goals while simultaneously convincing your subconscious that you already have achieved them is to organize your future goals by intertwining them with accomplishments from the past and current experiences. The reason being is that your subconscious does a lousy job of conceptualizing time. So, by intertwining things you're grateful for that have already happened, you can draw on the emotions you felt in that moment. You've already felt them, and the gratitude for having them already. The same principle applies to whatever good is happening in the present because you know what it feels like. So, when you express gratitude for something you want in the future, your subconscious is tricked into feeling like you already have it.

You might be asking why if your subconscious thinks you already have something, why would you consciously take action to get it? Your conscious mind knows you don't have something yet, but it doesn't matter. If your subconscious believes something is true, it will try to figure out how to make it true. You must trust the process.

To give you an example, let's say that you already have children, you are currently employed somewhere, and you want a new truck in the future. Your piece of paper would say something like:

I'm grateful for...
My wonderful children
Having a job with steady income
My brand new truck

Now, I mentioned that I like to write these on the back of a business card, laminate it, and put it in my pocket. The reason I do this is not only so I can have it handy to read in the morning and the evening, but so I can sometimes periodically read it throughout my day as well. On top of that, whenever I reach for something in my pocket like ChapStick, or my keys and I touch that card, the sensation of touch sends a little signal up my fingers and arm to my brain that reminds me of what's on that card. My brain knows what's on that card, and it keeps it in the forefront of my mind. Remember how I said that we get what we focus on in life?

One of the biggest obstacles to this is that people tend to focus on what they don't want. They do this by not necessarily thinking about how great it would be to have achieved their goal. They tend to think about how crappy their current situation is instead. It's not the same thing at all. Using the truck example again, let's say you currently drive a 2010 Dodge Nitro and continually have issues with it. Instead of thinking how great it will be to have less problems with your brand-new truck, you keep thinking about how many problems your Nitro has. You think if it's not one thing it's another with this crappy Dodge! Are you thinking about the new truck when you do that, or are you thinking about the Dodge? Your subconscious only hears Dodge, and you keep getting more of that damned Dodge! Instead, when you have problems with your Dodge, you need to stop for a minute and think about how great it will be to have that new truck. Sure, take care of the issues with the Dodge, but be thankful that you'll soon have a new truck, and your focus will change.

This comes down to awareness. Before reading this, you most likely never realized that your thoughts had such an outcome on your experience in life. Keep this in mind because your perception of things shapes your reality. A lot of people who hear about The Law of Attraction become concerned that they may think the wrong thing and it will interfere with or block what they are trying to achieve. The good news is that this isn't the case. If you have awareness of your thoughts, and where they are being directed, you can make corrections and get your mind focused back on what you actually want, and not on what you don't want.

Another thing that I think is important to point out is that I purposefully used *I'm grateful for...* at the beginning of your goal list. There's a very important reason for this. You see, practicing what I like to call an *attitude of gratitude*, or feeling grateful for the things you have, helps to put you in the right mental state to achieve your goals. This includes feeling grateful for the things you want, but visualizing what it's like to already have what you want. I can't stress enough that the feeling of gratitude is paramount if you want to see any results in your life.

Up to this point you might be thinking this is a load of hogwash, magical woo-woo thinking, or whatever. I completely understand that. However, there is a reason I used the Toyota Tundra TRD Pro as an example of a new truck for a goal, and the 2010 aging Dodge Nitro as the current vehicle. Because I currently have a Toyota Tundra TRD Pro, and I used to have a shitty Dodge Nitro. Not only that, I focused on the Toyota Tundra so much, especially when my Nitro would have issues, that I eventually got one. Plus, I paid for it in cash. The cash came at the perfect time too. It was a lump sum payout for stock options I had when the company I work for was acquired. It coincidentally happened right before my Nitro finally broke down for good. So now I own my Tundra outright with no payments, and I no longer have that damned Nitro!

One might say that's a very fortunate coincidence, and I would agree if that sort of thing only happened once or twice. If it continually happens, then I find it hard to believe it is only a coincidence.

I also got the house I live in in a similar way, all in the perfect time. I've had big names on my weekly podcast, *Come On Man*, because I've focused on meeting the right people. Initially, I didn't know how I was going to be able to afford my house, or get in contact with the guests I've had, but somehow my subconscious figured it out.

For the house, I focused on having one for months and it turned out that I made enough to qualify for a loan. On top of that, my credit score was good enough to get the loan with a very low interest rate. All I had to do was talk to a realtor about it, and my realtor randomly showed up one day in the timeline of my Facebook feed. She wasn't just any realtor either, but the realtor who was selling some houses I would walk by every day when I would walk my dog.

I would walk by some houses that were being built, and every day I would look at the houses, wonder if I could afford one and look at the realtor sign in front. I would imagine living in those homes, or at least my own home. My focus would always be drawn to that particular realtor's signs. I don't recall being overly focused on other realtor's signs. Right near the end of the Covid-19 lockdowns in 2020, those houses popped up on my Facebook feed from a post by my realtor. I took it as a sign that I needed to reach out to her, and I did.

It turns out that I didn't like those houses that were being built, but the very next morning after meeting her to look at them, I received a call from my landlord's wife. I had never spoken to her before, but she let me know that she and her husband were going to sell the house I was renting. Again, I took this as a sign that it was time to take action on buying my house, so I called the realtor and told her although I wasn't interested in the homes she showed me, I needed her to put me in a house quickly.

This was on a Tuesday morning, and she scheduled showings for me for the following Friday and Saturday. On Friday I walked into my current home, and it was perfect. We looked at several other homes, but the one I live in now was my first pick. I told her to make an offer for it at $10,000 under the asking price. I remember thinking at the time that if the sellers accepted the offer without negotiating, it would be a miracle. The realtor called back the next day letting me know they accepted the offer!

When it comes to my podcast guests, it's a much simpler process. Initially, I would just set out an intention for a specific guest, and I would randomly get ideas on ways I could potentially contact them. This happened a lot, so I won't get into a lot of stories about how I managed to get all of my guests on the show, but I will tell you about one particular guest. His name is Dr. Robert Glover, and a lot of what you will learn in the dating and relationship-related chapters came from things I learned from him.

I had an intention of interviewing Dr. Robert Glover because his work in his books **No More Mr. Nice Guy** and **Dating Essentials For Men** were very influential on me and changed the way I saw healthy relationships.

One day I noticed that a friend of mine who had a YouTube channel had Dr. Robert Glover on his show. I took it as a sign. I immediately reached out asking how he was able to get in contact with Dr. Robert Glover. His response was simple, he went to Dr. Glover's website and there is a contact form there. It was so simple, I wanted to slap myself in the face.

I decided to do the same thing. I went to Dr. Glover's website and used the contact form, and several months later Dr. Glover emailed me back and sent me a link to schedule the interview with him. To this day, his interview is one of the most popular episodes of my show.

You can use The Law of Attraction to achieve literally anything you want in life. You can use it to achieve the body you want, the partners you want, the friends you want, the job you want. You're only limited by what you believe can become your reality.

If you want to go in-depth on this, and how you can use this in your life, I highly recommend you check out my Practical Law of Attraction course at **http://loa.comeonmanpod.com**!

EDUCATION

When I was growing up both my parents beat it into me that I wouldn't be anything in life without at least a bachelor's degree from college. My mom was a critical care nurse for thirty years. She herself didn't even have a bachelor's degree. She got into nursing when all you needed was an associate degree. My dad didn't have a degree at all. He said he attended a semester of college at Metro State in Denver and decided that college wasn't for him. He opted to go to a trade school instead for computer programming. He attended DIT, the Denver Institute of Technology, which got bought out by ITT Tech in the late 80's or early 90's.

When my dad met my mom, he was working as a computer operator for the hospital my mom worked at, and they met in the break room. They ended up dating for a few months before rushing to get married. Their excuse was that they weren't getting any younger. My dad was 29 and my mom was 28.

My dad eventually left his job at the hospital and went to work for a big company called Mid-Continent. To this day, I'm not sure exactly what they did. All I know was that he ran the old punch-card computer systems for them on computers that took up entire rooms and stored data on tape reels. I also don't know how long he worked for them before he was eventually laid off. That company went out of business, but also the technology he was running was becoming obsolete and was slowly being replaced with smaller, faster computers.

My dad ended up going into depression after the layoff, and he was out of work for quite some time. At this point, my brother and I were very little, and my mom had stopped nursing to be a stay-at-home mom. Because my dad got laid off and couldn't snap out of his depression to find a new gig, she had to go back to nursing and became the major breadwinner for the family. Let me tell you, she NEVER let my brother and I forget it, either!

After months of being out of work, my dad finally found a job working for a heating and air conditioning repair company. He did that for a few years before he resigned due to issues with his paychecks. His boss was notorious for not paying employees on time, and my dad had enough of it. He told my brother and I that if a company messes with your paycheck more than twice in a row, that you should quit that company right there without notice because they are incompetent.

When my dad quit this time, I don't remember him going into a depression. I also don't remember him being out of work too long. I don't recall how long it took him, but he eventually got hired on as a temporary custodian for the local school district, where he ended up making it a career.

If you don't know, a custodian is a fancy word for janitor. You might look down on such a position, but let me tell you, this worked out very well for my mom and dad. As a custodian for the school district, he worked for the local government. Government jobs don't often pay a whole lot on the front end, but they pay off in the long run on the backend with pensions. To this day my parents are living off his pension even though my mom was the breadwinner while they both worked. All the money she saved for retirement is being drawn on and being re-invested in a money market account. My dad played the long game.

Now, I'm telling you all of this because it helped shape my worldview growing up when it came to education. The story my parents told me was that because neither of my parents earned their bachelor's degrees in college, they ended up struggling to make ends meet. Because I saw it all around me, I believed it as well. So, I knew I had to go to college eventually to get a bachelor's degree so I wouldn't struggle like they did.

This was the primary driver for me to join the US Navy out of high school. I remember sitting on the chest fly machine in my weight training class. I realized that real life was coming soon, and I needed to figure out a game plan. I **HAD** to go to college to get a bachelor's degree, but neither my parents nor I had the money to pay for college. I also wanted to get the hell out of my parents' house but wasn't sure how I would pay bills and make ends meet. It all seemed so monumental at the time.

I realized that I had several cousins in the military already, and they seemed to be doing well. As I started thinking about it more, I realized that the military would feed me, house me, pay me, and even offer college money in the form of the Montgomery GI Bill for veterans! This became my game plan. I would join the military, move out of my parents' house, let Uncle Sam show me the world, and I would go to college after the fact!

That is exactly what I did. I ended up spending four years in the US Navy a majority of that was stationed on the USS Shiloh (CG-67), and when I finished my enlistment, I ended up graduating from the now defunct Coleman University with a bachelor's degree in network security and a bachelor's degree in computer networks.

Here is where my worldview was fundamentally changed when it comes to education. You see when I was getting out of the Navy, I had to attend a class called Transition Assistance Program, or TAP. TAP is essentially a class that teaches you how to be a civilian again. We learned things like how to interview and how to write resumes. One of my TAP instructors told us that employers don't care about education and that they only care about experience. He went on to tell us that our military training gave us all sorts of experience that employers wanted. He also said that when employers list out job requirements for a position, it's just a glorified wish list, and we should apply whether we meet all of the qualifications or not.

I didn't believe that instructor initially when he was telling us all of this. I mean, I watched my parents struggle for twenty-two years up until this point. They said that I wouldn't struggle if I went out and got my bachelor's degree. I HAD TO GET MY BACHELOR'S DEGREE!

Here's the thing, though. While I was going to college, I got my first internship position in Information Technology. I got that position because my wife at the time had a college friend of her own, and that college friend was married to a guy who was the Help Desk manager for Websense in San Diego, CA. My wife invited them over to a party once, and simply asked her friend's husband if he had any jobs available. She told him that I was going to school for computers. We got to know each other at the party, and he liked me, so he essentially created a position for me. I got the job, and my foot in the door in Information Technology due to networking, NOT necessarily because of my education!

In fact, every single job I've had in the Information Technology world has been because I knew somebody. Sure, that only gets you so far. I mean, it was my job knowledge and charisma during interviews that landed me the jobs, but knowing people got my foot in the door for interviews. Knowing people got my resume pushed to the top of the list. The job knowledge itself didn't even come from my college education, it came from on-the-job training and self-study for certifications.

At the time of this writing, I've climbed the ladder to a senior director position for the company I currently work for. One might think that the bachelor's degrees that I earned helped get me there, but let me tell you, I know plenty of other guys in the industry at the same or even higher positions who never went to college. They learned everything from on-the-job training, tinkering on computers at home, or self-studying to get certifications that cost way less than a college degree.

The moral of the story is you don't necessarily need to get a bachelor's degree to be successful. My parents were fundamentally wrong about that.

I have several industry certifications under my belt. The most expensive ones cost about $300 or so, and my employers paid for them. I have never spent a dime on my own certifications, but even if I had, that money would have been better spent than the $40,000+ I spent on my dual bachelor's degrees, and probably would have gotten me just as far. They certainly wouldn't have put me in tens of thousands of dollars of student loan debt! That debt is all paid off now, but you get my point.

All this being said, let's talk about college for a bit. Don't get me wrong. There are certain circumstances in which formal education is necessary. On top of that, there's a smart way to go to college that most people don't think about too often. This is the plan I will outline for you.

You should only go to college if the career you want to go into requires it. For instance, you cannot become a Physician or a Surgeon without going to college. It used to be that you could become an attorney by simply taking the bar exam and passing it. That is no longer the case. You must go to college if you want to be an attorney. If the career you want requires it, go to college.

If you want to be a farmer, you don't have to go to college. If you want to be an auto mechanic, you don't have to go to college. If you want to be a rough-necker and work the oil rigs, you absolutely don't need college. In fact, oil rig workers make an epic ton of money compared to other professions! Hell, you can become a computer programmer without going to college and they make a lot of money too! They easily make six figures or more. If you're really good, you can write your own program and sell it for millions! Zero college is required, and you can even teach yourself programming.

You don't even need to spend money on certifications for that.

Going to college, getting a degree, and taking on tens of thousands of dollars in student loan debt for jobs that don't require it is just a stupid thing to do. Some people say you should go for the *college experience*, but you need to ask yourself if drunken frat parties are worth tens of thousands of dollars in debt. The answer to that is absolutely not! Besides, you can go to drunken frat parties for free. You don't even need to be enrolled in college.

On that note, let's go off on a tangent for a minute. When I was in the Navy, I went home on leave one time and went up to Fort Collins to hang out with some friends from high school. They took me to a frat party at Colorado State University that was off the hook! They had ice sculpture shots and hot sorority chicks everywhere. They even had the cops called on them, and we had to get out of there quickly! It was awesome, and I wasn't even a student there nor was I a member of the fraternity.

You should be catching my drift when it comes to not needing college, but let's say you want to get into a career that requires it. For instance, my daughter wants to be an attorney. She will have to go to college to become one. There really is no avoiding it. There is, however, a smarter way of doing it so that she doesn't get too far into debt. Here's how:

First, go to a community college for the first two years. Now, you might have the idea that you will only get hired by law firms if you go to a prestigious school like Harvard or Yale. You would be mistaken. More on that in a bit. You can always finish your degree at a good university, but it's ridiculously expensive to start at a university and take all the general education bullshit classes you are required to take in order to be "well rounded." You're much better off knocking out the first two years of bullshit classes at a much less expensive community college and transfer those credits to university later when you are ready to actually start taking classes for your career.

A lot of community colleges are cheap enough that you don't have to take out student loans to attend. When I was going to community college, it only cost eleven dollars per credit to go! It was so cheap that I was able to pay for it out of pocket with my crappy security guard job. You might be asking why I didn't use my G.I. Bill money on that. Well, I was drawing on my G.I. Bill, but we were using it to pay for my wife's tuition since she was going to San Diego State at the time. Yes, my G.I. Bill went to pay for my now ex-wife's education. It was stupid in hindsight. The point is that many community colleges can be paid for out of pocket if you work a full-time job at the same time. It takes a little more effort to do that, but it's worth it in the long run. Besides, you'll still have a little time to yourself to enjoy life, especially if you get a job like I did that lets you work on schoolwork while on the job. Graveyard security guard gigs are perfect for that!

The next thing you need to know about college is that it really doesn't matter where you get your degree or how good your grades are. Most employers don't care. They just want you to have a degree.

I learned this because I transferred to Coleman University from San Diego State when I realized that San Diego State didn't have a degree in computer networks. I was initially pursuing a computer information systems degree at the recommendation of a college guidance counselor who didn't know shit about computers until I realized that it was more about programming than networks and systems administration which is what I wanted to do. You see, by this point, I had already been working for a few years in the information technology industry without having completed my degree. I already knew what I needed to know. I just wanted that piece of paper.

Coleman University was essentially a trade school, but it was accredited by ACICS to award degrees up to masters. I loved that school. They had what they referred to as an inverted curriculum where they taught you all of the skills you needed to get a job in information technology first, then you would take your bullshit "well rounded" classes later in associate's, bachelor's and master's levels. Since I had already gone through community college, and did some time at San Diego State, after the core program I jumped over associate's and went into the bachelor's program. I earned my dual bachelor's degrees because it only required one or two more classes. I added those classes and was awarded two degrees. It was like a two-for-one sale!

Since graduating, I've never had a potential employer scoff at the school or question its legitimacy. They just liked seeing that I had a bachelor's degree, even though as I've said before, I didn't need it. Hell, that school went out of business in 2018! Employers really don't care!

Another thing I've never been asked for are my transcripts! Employers don't care about what grades you earned to get your degree. They just care that you got your degree! Let me ask you a question. What do you call a doctor who graduated medical school with all C's? You call him a doctor. Do you see what I mean?

So, if your career requires you to go to college and get some sort of degree, first you'll want to knock out the first two years in community college, and then you will want to transfer to some sort of university. As I've already established, nobody cares what university you attend, so you might as well attend one that is somewhat affordable. Most state universities are less expensive than private universities. Check around and pick one that is the most affordable for you as long as it has the program, you'll need to get you into the field you want. A lot of them also offer a monthly tuition payment plan that could be affordable enough for you to pay out of pocket without having to get student loans.

For the rest of you who want to work in a career that doesn't require college, and that is a majority of you, you're better off finding a local trade school. Look into self-studying for industry certifications or try to find a local apprenticeship.

Trade schools are pretty much everywhere. I live in the middle of nowhere in rural Colorado, and we even have one here. They have programs for dental assisting, medical assisting, medical coding, welding, HVAC repair, electrical contracting, truck driving, cosmetology, and phlebotomy. Other trade schools offer other programs as well.

All of those are good jobs that pay decently and can even get your foot in the door to bigger, better things. Jobs like welding and electrical contracting are so hard to fill now that those guys can make a really good living! The best part is trade schools are much less expensive than universities. Some of these schools offer certifications for as little as $10,000 compared to at least $40,000 for a bachelor's degree. It may seem expensive, but you'll pay that off in no time with your salary from your new higher-paying job. Moreover, a lot of these programs can be completed in just a few months.

If the Job you want doesn't require a degree or certification from a trade school, that leaves careers where you can learn through self-study. Most jobs in systems administration, network administration, network security, and even software development don't require trade school or college. You can fill your resume with industry certifications instead, and most of those are only a few hundred bucks a piece. You can even take courses for extremely reasonable rates online. You don't even have to do that though because there are so many books available for just about every certification you want.

One issue with certifications and college degrees, though, is that they really don't mean anything at the end of the day. They all look really nice on your resume. They may even make your resume stand out compared to the next guy, but they won't get you the job by themselves. They will only get your foot in the door. It's what you know and oftentimes who you know that actually gets you the position you want. So my TAP instructor was right all along. Experience and knowledge will often trump any degree or certification more often than not.

We've come all this way, and we really haven't talked about education yet. You're probably scratching your head right about now. Allow me to elaborate. All of the things above about college degrees, trade schools and certifications aren't REALLY education. Those systems are designed to show you how to pass tests and satisfy requirements. Real education is not necessarily about passing tests and satisfying requirements. Real education is obtaining knowledge and having a true and thorough understanding of a subject.

When it comes to your career, your real education will result from doing the job itself, not reading a book about it and taking a test. The truth is, you don't need a college or certification to gain knowledge and have a true understanding of something. My dad used to tell me growing up that everything you ever want to know can be found in a book. He's absolutely right about that, and I'll take it one step further: everything you ever want to know can also be found online. There are videos on YouTube, blog articles, online encyclopedias like Wikipedia, for instance. It's all out there and for the most part it's all free.

Going back to books, even those are free. You can find free books at your local library; hell, you may have found this book at your local library. My favorite books are audiobooks because you can listen to them everywhere you go. I like to listen to audiobooks while out running, when I'm driving my car, or even when I'm doing yard work. A friend of mine once called audiobooks "effortless learning."

One thing I learned about books is that we typically only retain about 10% of what we read, so if you really want to master something in a book, you should read it at least 10-15 times! I'm not saying you should read this book that many times, but if you really want to retain everything I say, then that's what you should do.

An interesting thing I learned about reading books multiple times is that you almost always find something in the book you didn't notice before. Some people call it an "a*h ha* moment." Bob Proctor, of the **Proctor Gallagher Institute** says it's because as you're reading along, your mind starts to wander at different points while you are contemplating an idea. You are still reading along, but you aren't really paying attention. Each time you read a book, your mind wanders on tangents at different times, so when your attention comes back to the book, you often come back to a point where your mind was wondering previously. It sort of makes sense if you think about it.

Another interesting thing I've found when reading a particular book many times, and I'm talking the 15+ times mark, is that the material starts to become a part of you. It starts to shape your thoughts, personality, and overall viewpoint. It's almost like brainwashing. Putting it that way sounds bad, but it can actually be a good thing if the material in the book is positive and helps you to become a better person. There are a few books in my multi-read rotation that have that impact on me. All of them will be listed at the end of the book.

The one thing that books will never do though is give you experience. Going back to my TAP instructor, nothing really trumps experience. You can have all the college degrees in the world, you can read one book a thousand times, but it all means nothing if you don't go out and practice what you are learning yourself. If you don't go out and practice, it's all just theory.

If you are a motivated person like me, you can teach yourself literally everything you ever want to know or do. It's just like my dad said. I'm the kind of person who doesn't really need a coach or a mentor as long as I have books on a particular subject. The reason why is that I'm not afraid to go out and try what I'm learning. I'm also not afraid to evaluate what worked and what didn't, or what I could improve on. I am self-motivated.

A lot of people hire coaches and mentors because they need someone to motivate them to do something, hold them accountable if they don't, and to help them evaluate what they are doing wrong. If you are one of those people, don't fret! There is nothing wrong with that either. Through my podcast, I've met lots of coaches and mentors. They are a wealth of knowledge and can seriously help you accomplish whatever you want in life. If you need someone to push you, I highly recommend investing money in a coach or a mentor. It's certainly money better spent than on worthless degrees like underwater basket weaving or gender studies.

I offer one-on-one coaching myself. If you need help in any area in this book, you can work with me directly by visiting **http://comeonmanpod.com** and signing up for one of my coaching programs.

So, let's sum this up. Unlike what my parents told me, you don't need to go to college in order to be successful in life. You only really need college if the career you want requires it. Trade schools and industry certifications will probably be more than enough to land you a decent-paying job that you can be proud of and find satisfaction in. You can self-educate from books and online materials for almost no money, and probably get a better education than you would from a university. On top of that, you can study the topics you actually care about. Finally, if you really want to get to the next level, hiring a coach or a mentor might not be a bad idea.

CAREER

With the last chapter on education, we've already talked a little about careers, but now we're going to go in-depth. In most Western cultures, your career defines you as a person. People often shape their viewpoints on you based on your career. It also shapes your identity as perceived by yourself and others.

For instance, when people ask you what you do for a living, you don't say "I do accounting" if you are an accountant. You don't typically say "I practice medicine" if you are a doctor. No, you say I am an accountant, or I am a physician. Saying *I AM* anything is identifying as that thing.

So, if you are going to identify as something, and it is going to have a profound impact on your identity and how people perceive you, then shouldn't you take some time thinking about what is right for you to do?

Another thing you should consider when choosing the right career is what you really want out of life. Do you want to travel the world? Do you want to be able to work in your pajamas from home? Do you want to be filthy rich? Answering questions like these will help you determine the right career path. When you sit down and think about what you really want, you might find that being a lawyer or a politician isn't exactly the right path you should take.

In this chapter, I am going to give you some things to think about that you may not have otherwise thought of. You can take these into consideration when choosing your career path. Some of these things your high school guidance counselor won't tell you, because high school guidance counselors are a part of the machine, and they just want to turn out more cogs to join them in the machine. Most guidance counselors will push you towards college so you can get into student loan debt and keep the machine working. If that's what you want to do, cool. That just might not be the right path for you when you sit down and think about it.

Let's start with the route I took coming out of high school. I joined the US Navy. I remember vividly to this day when I decided to do that. I was sitting on the chest fly machine in the basement of Evergreen High School in Evergreen, Colorado during weight training class. It was my senior year, and it dawned on me that life was coming at me fast and I didn't have enough money to go to college. I also wasn't making enough in my part time job at the grocery store. On top of that, I was raised that people who live with their parents after high school are losers. How was I going to be able to live on my own as well as afford college?

Then it clicked! I had cousins in the military, so why don't I join the military myself? They will give me a salary, free healthcare, job training, a place to sleep, food to eat, and lots of other benefits including paying for college with the Montgomery G.I. Bill. I would also be eligible for other college incentives depending on the job I qualify for when I join. And not just me, but you, too. Yes, they will give you ALL of that, plus you get to see the world!

Having served in the military, I am one of those crotchety old veterans who thinks that every kid coming out of high school should serve at least one tour in the military. Other countries, like Israel, do it. I'm not saying that we should do it because they do it. No, I think it's a great idea because it lets you move out of your parent's house for a bit under the care of good old Uncle Sam. You obtain good life skills, and you get to see what the real world is like. You don't typically get that sort of thing when you go to college. In college, you're more likely to get indoctrinated in left-wing ideology than to experience what it's like in other countries.

Another thing you can think about when it comes to the military option is that pretty much any job you could ever want to do, you can do it in the military. Want to be a chef someday? Cool, you can join as a mess specialist. Want to be a singer? Did you know the Navy has a musician rate? I'm not joking at all. Look it up!

Now you might be laughing at the chef vs mess specialist idea but consider this for a minute. When I served, our mess department had a Senior Chief Mess Specialist who oversaw all the cooks, including the cooks for the officers. When he left the ship I was on, his next assignment was the White House where he was the personal chef for President George W. Bush!

A lot of people are afraid to join the military because they are afraid they might see some action. If that's your concern, then consider joining the US Navy where you will most likely be stationed on a ship, and there are pretty much zero naval battles anymore. You are well out of harm's way where you will simply push a button to blow up the bad guys from hundreds of miles away.

Or, you could join the US Air Force where most of those guys live in air conditioned tents, mess with radio communications, and look at maps all day. They aren't rucking it in the desert with machine guns like Soldiers or Marines. It's essentially a 9-5 gig most of the time.

Long story short, even if you don't want to make the military a career, it can certainly give you a leg up in important job and life skills that you wouldn't otherwise get. You absolutely should consider it as an option to make sure you succeed in life.

Military or not, you really should consider what you want your life to look like in ten years, twenty years, and further. Do you imagine yourself hiking in the mountains of Colorado in your spare time? Do you imagine yourself snorkeling with dolphins in the ocean? Do you want to travel the world and have the freedom and income to afford to do all of that? All of this needs to be considered before picking your career.

You see, there are plenty of people who get out of high school and either their parents or guidance counselor tell them what they should be. They should be an accountant because they are good at math. They should be a nurse because they like taking care of people. However, choosing a career path because someone else thought you might be good at it is one of the dumbest things ever. You should choose to do something because you really like doing it, and it gives you the lifestyle you want to live. Remember The Law of Attraction in the first chapter? This is part of it!

You should sit down and write out what you want to accomplish in your life. You should doodle it and draw pictures of it. You should hang up cork boards in your bedroom, and tack pictures of the places you want to see on it, and things you want to own. You want to study these things every day because your subconscious will work night and day to figure out how to make it a reality. If this concept hasn't clicked yet, go back and read the first chapter.

On top of what you want your lifestyle to look like, you should also consider what you enjoy doing and what you hate doing. I personally hate cleaning, so working at restaurants or anywhere that needed custodians was out of the question. When I got out of the Navy, I loved to surf the internet all day. I ended up getting into information technology where I could work on the networks and servers that are essentially the backbone of the internet itself. I absolutely love it, too! When you love what you do, you can't really consider it work.

Some people will tell you to make your passion your career, and while that may work for a few people, it's rare that you can make your hobby monetizable enough to live off of. It's not impossible, just highly improbable. A more rational thing to say then is that you should find a career path that you enjoy rather than try to make your hobby your career. If both can be done, that's just icing on the cake!

Ok, so while you are thinking about what you want to do for the rest of your life, let's consider some professions you might enjoy and that can give you the freedom and flexibility to do what you want to do.

Anything that can be done remotely is my first recommendation. As I mentioned before, I got into information technology. In 2013, my now ex-wife wanted to move back to Colorado. We were living in California at the time, and we both hated it there. Without getting too political, let's just say that when we moved back to Colorado, I felt like a political refugee. I had asked the company I work for if I could do my job remotely from Colorado. They agreed to it for a ninety-day probationary period to see if I could make it work. At the time of this writing, which was nine years ago, I'm still going strong.

When the COVID-19 pandemic happened in 2020, my whole company went remote. A lot of other companies went remote as well, and now it's even easier to find remote work in pretty much any profession thanks to the Internet and Zoom calls.

The cool thing about working remotely is that you have more flexibility to get stuff done around the house. For instance, I'll run a load of laundry in between meetings, or go bang out a few sets on my home gym. If I need to run to the store or go watch one of my kids have a school assembly, I can do that real quick and nobody cares! The important thing when working remotely is making sure you hit your deadlines. As long as you are getting your work done, everybody is happy, and they won't question what you are doing. At this point in my life, I don't think I could ever go back to a permanent office gig full-time. I'd go absolutely nuts!

If you want even more flexibility, you could do freelance work instead. This is where having a skill comes in handy. I know plenty of guys in the information and technology fields who run their own consulting businesses full-time. They just have a bunch of clients they service instead of one employer. They set their own hours, and only take on as much work as they can handle.

I know developers who do nothing but Fiverr and Upwork gigs. In fact, I've hired people on Fiverr to do work for my podcast including professional voice talent. Tune into an episode of **Come On Man** on your favorite podcast platform. You hear that guy at the opening? He cost me $100 on Fiverr. So yes, you can be a professional voice talent assuming the demand is high enough to make a living wage with.

Not all jobs are very conducive to freelance or remote work, but they are still great careers.

Maybe you like working on cars? Auto mechanics can make six figures if they know what they are doing and work for the right shops. My brother is one. Although mechanics are hourly, they are actually paid by the job. You see, replacing an engine is estimated at a certain number of hours of work. So is replacing spark plugs, putting on a timing belt, etc. If you can get those jobs done faster than the time estimated, you get paid for the full estimate. It incentivizes mechanics to work fast, because the faster they get the work done, the more money they make.

The real money in any industry is owning your own business, though. Owning your own business is a faster method to build wealth, and many of these skill-based careers can be turned into businesses. I know mechanics in my area who run their own mobile car service businesses. I know the actual owners of some of the shops in my area. The owners make way more than the people who work for them do in most cases.

Some jobs sound good, but you have no freedom.

Have you heard of oilfield roughnecks? Those guys work on oil rigs and make a boat load of money. The big drawback to it is that they are almost never home. There are a lot of oilfield families where I live, and the wives are here with the kids most of the year in their huge houses while their husbands are gone months at a time. If you don't like being away from your family for months at a time, or you don't want your wife shacking up with the UPS guy, then perhaps the money isn't worth it for a job like this.

I could go on and on about various jobs and their benefits or lack of benefits, but, again, it really comes down to the lifestyle you want to live and whether that job will get you where you want to go in the long run. I'm just using these as examples of jobs you might not have considered otherwise. Some jobs are just good for a certain skill set that you can carry over to other jobs. More on that in a little bit.

This is all great, but how do you land your dream job, or get your foot in the door? All sorts of kids come out of college these days and complain that they can't get the job they want. All employers want experience, so how do they get experience? I hate to burst your bubble, but the reason these people can't get the experience they need is because they aren't willing to put the work in.

You see, obtaining experience looks a whole lot like work. These people who complain think they are owed a job simply because they wrote some papers in school and memorized enough stuff to pass an exam. Remember what my TAP instructor told me when I got out of the Navy? He said that employers don't care about degrees. They care about experience. I'll tell you how you can get some.

First, every single job I got in my professional career was largely because of WHO I knew, not necessarily WHAT I knew. My now ex-wife was good at networking. She has a naturally bubbly personality, and she's not afraid to introduce herself to new people and try to get to know them. In college, she also liked to join clubs to meet people and network. During college, she met a gal who was married to the help desk manager at a company that used to be called Websense.

My now ex-wife once invited her and her husband over to our apartment for a party. During that party my wife casually asked her friend's husband if he had any entry level jobs available. I was working at a factory at the time, but I was going to college for computer information systems. Actually, that was just my major. I was still doing all of my general education stuff in community college. I had zero computer experience, really. I could do basic stuff like use Excel and Word, but not much else. He didn't know that though. She just said I was in school for "computers."

A few weeks later, my now ex-wife's friend called her to say that her husband had a job for me. It was called Information Technology Auditor. He basically made it up and got approval for it. It was essentially a paid internship. My job was to walk around the offices all day and clean people's keyboards and mice as well as make sure their computers had the latest updates from Microsoft.

In my downtime, I would hang out with the desktop and help desk technicians where I would learn how to replace RAM, hard drives and motherboards. I eventually caught a really "big" break around Christmas time when I volunteered to sit at the help desk and take calls so the full time help desk folks could take time off. It was here that I really learned how to troubleshoot issues over the phone and got real experience.

I also took advantage of the company's certification program. They would pay for your certification test, including one failure. I would spend hours a day at work in between my regular duties studying for certifications. When I was ready to test, I'd ask my boss to schedule an exam for me.

I want you to think of professional certifications like fake boobs. Women will often get their current husband to pay for their fake boobs, but it is their next boyfriend who gets to play with them! Same thing for certifications. If your current employer will pay for them, take full advantage of it. It will look good on your resume, so when review time comes you can either ask for a raise or take your shiny new certifications to another employer and let them play with them…for a higher salary, of course.

Another thing I did when I was at Websense was that I started doing a home computer repair side hustle via Craigslist for extra money and experience. A few of the other guys I was working with were doing it, and it turned out to be lucrative. I was only charging $50 per hour because I was still a newbie, but some of these guys were charging a few hundred and had retainers with doctors' offices.

Let me tell you about home computer users. Nobody fucks up computers like home users. Home users also have the nasty habit of keeping ancient relics around that are obsolete and you can't buy parts for. They also have no idea what antivirus is. They buy a computer from Staples, it comes with a 90 day free trial of McAfee, and they think they are good to go. Meanwhile, after years of porn watching and who knows what else, their computers are riddled with viruses.

I used to go to people's houses with a CD full of free software, including a free Antivirus called AVG. I think they're still around. AVG was great, and, again, it was free. I would literally install a free software that anyone could download themselves, and manually kick off a scan. I would sit there while it scanned, sometimes for two to three hours. All the while getting paid. I was getting paid to run free software.

At first, I had some moral questions about it, but after discussing it with my colleagues at my day job, they assured me that the clients weren't paying me for the free software.

They were paying for my expertise! There's a big difference there, and you should take note of that.

When I left Websense, my next job was secured because while I was interviewing for a help desk position, one of my former colleagues from Websense was now working there and he vouched for me. It also helped that by this time, I really knew my shit.

I had been working at Websense's help desk for a few years, and our call center would get about six hundred calls a day. This new place, we would get maybe forty on a busy day. Working in this slower-paced environment after having been through a hellaciously-paced environment made me look like Superman. I was closing cases faster than any of the other help desk guys. In fact, I would go into their queues and start working on stale cases they had. My bosses saw this and decided to promote me to Systems Administrator.

I ended up getting poached away from that job by a former manager of mine from Websense who was working with another Websense buddy of mine. They gave me a Sr. Systems Engineer position at the new place. I had basically made Sr. Systems Engineer in four years! Sure, a lot of it was talent, but most of it came down to who I knew.

I left that gig a few years later for my current employer. My friend from the last job had left due to personal issues and was offered a position at my current employer. He found something he liked better but told them about me and said I had all of the same certifications and experience. They called me up, and after talking with me for about thirty minutes, offered me the job for the same salary they had offered him.

I've been with that company for twelve years now and make a very good living.

The first lesson from my experience is that you need to start networking. You need to find local professional meetups that include people in the field you want to get into. My realtor who sold me my house used to put on a monthly business owner meetup in my local town so professionals could get together and network. That kind of thing is very powerful.

The second lesson is that you should hop on any opportunity to get your foot in the door of the industry you want to work in. If I had turned down the Information Technology Auditor position because *I knew my worth* and wanted to hold out for a high paying job out of school, I would probably still be working at that factory! I was willing to clean keyboards for an opportunity to fill in at the help desk on occasion.

The third lesson in this story is that if you are not finding the experience you need at your current employer, start a side hustle and make experience for yourself. If you want to be a web developer, get an old computer and build your own web server. Play with it. Troubleshoot it, then start a Fiverr gig and do it for other people. Even experiences you create for yourself can be added to your resume. Believe me, I put my Craigslist side hustle experience on my resume.

Let's continue this discussion about side hustles for a minute because there's another thing, I want you to think about. You see, when I was growing up, my parents would tell me that I should find a career in an industry that is recession-proof. My mom was a nurse, and there would always be sick people. My dad was a custodian, so there would always be a need for people who clean. My brother ended up being an auto mechanic. People would always need their cars repaired. I got into computers because, like it or not, our whole world runs on computers. In fact, if you are listening to this on audio or reading this on a tablet, THIS BOOK is on a computer!

In addition to your job being recession-proof, it also needs to be government lockdown-proof. We learned this in 2020 when state and local governments shut down businesses in the name of public safety. Whether that was a bit of an overreaction for a virus that had a 99.99% survival rate or not is for another book. The point is, when the government decides that you can't work, you don't want to get ruined the way a lot of people did.

I was lucky in that my company was considered essential, so I never lost a day of work. Lots of other people were not so lucky. The thing is though, I knew from my time at Websense that if push came to shove, I could side hustle my way through times like that. People ALWAYS need their computers, even during a pandemic. I could easily go door to door offering my services. In fact, while hair salons and barber shops were shut down, I knew hairdressers that would do that very thing. Or they set up salons in their houses to keep money coming in. Skills like this are paramount during a situation like we had in 2020.

Speaking of door-to-door jobs, let me tell you about the time I did door-to-door office supply sales. It was my second job after I left the Navy. I started working for a Multi-Level Marketing company called **DS Max**. It was a shitty job, but it taught me some valuable life skills that I think everyone should know. Namely, how to be friendly, outgoing, and how to sell. You see, everything in life is sales. I convinced you to buy this book, didn't I? If you agree with anything I'm saying in these chapters, it's because you are buying the ideas that I am selling. A lot of people think that selling and persuasion are dirty words, but they really aren't. If you do it right, you can get whatever you want out of life and make things mutually beneficial for those around you.

So, at this company, I would show up in a suit every morning for a rah-rah pump-up meeting. We would all hang out in a room with loud music playing, jumping around, teaching each other the 5 steps to a sale, the 4 impulse factors, or the 8 steps to success. Out of all of these things, the 4 impulse factors have stuck with me my whole life. Let me tell you the 5 steps to a sale though:

1. **Introduction** - Introduce yourself.
2. **Short Story** - Explain who you are and what you do.
3. **Presentation** - Explain your product and why they should buy.
4. **Close** - Assume the sale and ask for the order.
5. **Rehash** - Once they have agreed to the sale, try to get them to buy something else.

The 8 steps to success are:

1. **Have a great attitude.**
2. **Work your territory correctly.**
3. **Be on time.**
4. **Maintain your attitude.**
5. **Be prepared.**
6. **Know why you're there and what you're doing.**
7. **Work a full eight hours.**
8. **Take control.**

Those are self-explanatory. Finally, the 4 impulse factors are:

1. **Fear of loss** - This is where you tell people you have limited items, or they're only available for a limited time.
2. **Indifference** - This is where you act like you don't care if they buy or not.
3. **Greed** - This is where you tell people all of their friends are doing it. Everybody likes to keep up with the Joneses.
4. **Sense of urgency** – This is where you tell them to act now and remind them of the fear of loss.

The impulse factors are fascinating to watch in real time and are best to be used as part of your short story and presentation. It's hard to not look at all people the same when you see these psychological tricks work on most people.

While this job did suck, I did get pretty good at it. I was consistently closing deals and earning my commission-only checks, but it was really a matter of *feast or famine*. If I couldn't close deals, I wasn't eating. The problem with this particular sales job versus others was that we weren't allowed to build a pipeline. We were only allowed to make first-time sales. In other sales jobs you can make a sale then follow up with those customers down the road and foster a good business relationship. If you ever get offered a sales job and you aren't allowed to work your own pipeline, you might consider a different job.

Not being able to build and foster a sales pipeline can impact a salesman's income because they must rely on new sales to make commission. If you have a pipeline with customers you've worked with in the past who trust you, you can make more commissions through future sales.

The main point of this story, though, is that I learned how-to knock-on doors and make sales. I also learned how to manage rejection and get doors slammed in my face. A big thing we learned at this company was working what's called the *law of averages*. That essentially says that the more doors you knock on, the more sales you make. We used to say that the door we didn't knock was a sale that we missed. So, the job sucked, but the experience didn't. If there ever is another lockdown due to pandemic, like I said, I know how-to knock-on doors and sell my services. It wouldn't be a bad idea for you to learn the same. Especially if you want to sell your own services someday.

You don't need to wait to work for a door-to-door sales company to do this. You can go to a store, buy some candy bars and try to sell them door-to-door yourself. Maybe tell people you are raising money for school sports. The guys who started the door-to-door sales company I worked for got started by selling pots and pans they bought at Target out of their car trunks.

I've presented a lot of ideas for consideration in this chapter, but to summarize, the key takeaway is the importance of selecting a career that aligns with the lifestyle you aspire to. Additionally, acquiring skills that have broader applicability, especially in challenging situations like recessions or government lockdowns, is crucial. Money, while significant, shouldn't be the sole factor influencing your career choice. I discussed the military as a valuable option for gaining experience and exploring the world. The process of envisioning your desired life and then determining a career path to achieve that was emphasized. Enjoying your work is essential, as it transforms it from a chore to something fulfilling. Many jobs allow remote or freelance work, but some high-paying careers may lack freedom. Networking and gaining experience through internships or side hustles are valuable steps in securing jobs. Lastly, it's advisable to seek a job that is not only recession-proof but also resilient to government lockdowns.

ANYONE CAN GET RICH

This is one of my favorite subjects if I am going to be honest with you. If you bought this book because you follow me on social media, or you listen to my podcast *Come On Man*, you might think that my favorite topic is dating and relationships. While I do like discussing dating and relationships, I actually REALLY love building wealth and investing for retirement!

On top of that, this method that I am about to discuss can literally be used by anybody to retire as a millionaire if they start early enough. You're a retail worker? Yes, this will work for you. You work at McDonalds? Yes, this will work for you. The key to all of this is how early you start. If you are reading this as an eighteen-year-old kid coming out of high school, you better listen up! Because if you follow this plan, you can probably retire by your early to mid-40's if you play your cards right.

If you are just now reading this when you are over 40, and you haven't already done some of what I'm about to tell you, you might be in for a world of hurt. It might still be helpful, but you are going to struggle for retirement. That being said, I'll give you some suggestions on what to do that might make things work out. You won't like it though.

In order to give credit where credit is due, this whole entire section is loosely based off of Dave Ramsey's baby steps from his book, *Total Money Makeover*. I also got some things from Tony Robbins' book, *Money: Master The Game.* However, if you want to know the truth, Robbins' book is largely a rip-off of Dave's method. There were some slight differences, though, like how to allocate funds, using index funds instead of mutual funds, and setting your accounts to rebalance every year. Other than that, the steps are the same.

If you are familiar with Dave Ramsey's baby steps, I purposely leave out baby step 5 from my recommendation. That step is to save money for your kid's college tuition. The reason I leave that out is because I don't think parents should fund their children's college education. This isn't necessarily because I don't think they have to go to college as covered in my education chapter, but more because I don't think kids will respect their own education if mommy and daddy pay for it.

Almost everyone I know whose parents funded their college pissed it away and had to scramble to get their shit together to graduate. If your kids have to struggle and figure out how to pay their own way through college, they'll buckle down and study. They'll actually take their education seriously. Why? Because they are spending their own money on it. They have skin in the game!

Look at it like a bird's egg. If you have a bird that is struggling to get out of its eggshell, and you help it along by peeling back the shell, they oftentimes will die not long after. The baby birds need the struggle to be strong enough to survive on their own. The same goes with kids in college. They need that struggle in order to succeed in their college education, and eventually their chosen career field. Don't peel back the eggshell for them!

So with all of that being said, that leaves just 6 baby steps to wealth that you will take. Those are:

1. $1,000 emergency fund
2. Pay off debt using a "debt snowball"
3. Increase your emergency fund to 6 months' worth of savings
4. Invest 15% for retirement
5. Pay off your home early
6. Build wealth and give

If you are an 18 year old reading this book, some of these baby steps might not apply to you yet. No biggie, just skip them for now! In fact, if you don't have any debt at all, then you are ahead of the game on this one! Most people don't learn about debt in school, and most adults don't learn the difference between good debt and bad debt until they are trying to get out of bad debt! Still, some adults never learn.

As stated above, the sooner you start on this process in life, the better. That is because you are taking advantage of what is known as the time value of money. *Investopedia* defines this as:

> The time value of money (TVM) is the concept that a sum of money is worth more now than the same sum will be at a future date due to its earnings potential in the interim. This is a core principle of finance. A sum of money in the hand has greater value than the same sum to be paid in the future.

Essentially, it takes advantage of a feature called compound interest. Before I can explain what compound interest is, I have to explain what interest in general is. Let's say you invest $100 into the stock market, and you are getting a return on your investment in the form of dividends at a rate of 8% a year. That means your $100 earned an extra $8.

Compounding just means that you will now be paid both on the initial amount of your investment, but also the accumulated interest from previous periods. For example, now you have $108 in the stock market that is still paying you 8%. So the next year you will make 8% on your $108 which means you will make $8.64 the second year, bringing your total to $116.64. This will continue for as long as you have your money in the investment vehicle.

Using a simple compound interest calculator online, let's say you are 18 years old, and you save up and invest $6,000 in a Roth IRA, and contribute $500 per month for the next 40 years. Let's also assume you earn a rate of return at our original 8% annual return example. By the time you are 58 you will have $1,684,686.24.

See the graph below from **Investor.gov**:

A quick Google search at the time of this writing shows that the S&P 500 has actually seen an annual return of 9.4% on average for the last 50 years, so you could potentially have more than that. This is just an example to get you thinking about the power of compounding interest in the long term.

A large part of this method is also your ability to generate income. If you are 18 with no bills and no debt, you can certainly scratch together $500 per month to invest with your McDonalds job. However, if you do have bills and debts, this will be a struggle. That means that if you want to do this you have a few options:

1. Get a higher-paying job.

2. Make more money at your current job.
3. Get another job or side hustle.
4. Be a minimalist.

Number 4 is fine if you are a simple person who doesn't need a lot of extravagant things to be happy. I know plenty of people like this. My brother is an excellent example. He lives in a truck camper shell, showers at the gym, eats food from the local food bank and saves all of his money. I'm sure my brother is a millionaire at this point but lives like a total homeless person. He's happy though, so who am I to judge his lifestyle?

Living like that isn't for most people, though, so let's look at the other three options starting with the first one. Getting a higher paying job is certainly easier to do when you have specialty skills. To get those specialty skills you either need to go to some kind of school, or you need to learn on the job. Some higher paying jobs that don't require specialty education will offer on the job training.

For instance, after the Navy I worked at a production plant making pharmaceutical grade filter membranes. I was a rinse line operator. I got the job because a friend of my wife had a boyfriend who worked there doing quality control. He recommended me, I interviewed well, and they said they would train me. I made more at that job than I did at the private security job I was working at.

So here is a lesson for you, you can often make more money quicker if you leave your current job and go elsewhere. Sure, you can try to go with option 2 above and try to negotiate a raise, but the fact is most employers are willing to pay more for new talent than to increase wages of existing talent. Once I got into the information technology field, I found that I made money much faster by finding a new job every two years. It really doesn't benefit you to stay with a company for thirty years and retire anymore.

What about being loyal though? Most companies will drop you like a hot rock when it comes to cutting the budget. At my current job that I've been at for the last eleven years at the time of this writing, I've survived three sets of layoffs. The reason I survived is that I always kept my team lean and essential. Try having a company without an information technology department these days! The other people who weren't so lucky were expendable. All employees are expendable. If you died tomorrow morning, your employer would have a job posting on Monster by tomorrow afternoon. They are not loyal to you, so don't feel like you have to be loyal to them. Get your bag.

Wait, I stayed at this job for eleven years, but I'm recommending to leave every two? That doesn't make sense. Well, it does when you consider that I got divorced in that time period and when you do that, and your ex-wife wants to take you back to court every two years to try to get more money out of you, then it doesn't make sense to try to make more money. It's best to stay where you're at.

Another advantage of going elsewhere is the new employer doesn't necessarily know what you made at your last position, and they are not legally allowed to ask your previous employer. All they are allowed to ask is what your salary requirements are. This is huge because you can instantly give yourself a $10,000 or more a year raise if you want. Just be sure to look at what other people are making in your industry so you're being realistic. A great resource for this is salary.com.

You can find lots of online videos, books, and articles on salary negotiation. What I used to do when asked for my salary requirements was to tell potential employers that I'd prefer to discuss that if I am actually being seriously considered for the job. A lot of employers will take your salary requirement as a disqualifier so they can go with the lowest bidder. You want to make sure they are sincerely looking at you as one of their best options before bringing up money. Once I had confirmation that I was seriously in the running for the position, I'd tell them I was looking for a salary in a particular range.

So, let's say you are making $70,000 per year at your current position, and salary.com says that people with your job title in your area make in the range of $65,000 - $95,000. You're in the range, but you can certainly be making more. Then at your new potential employer, tell them that you will need something in the range of $90,000-$95,000 for you to leave your current employer. If they bite, this will put you near the top of the range for your area! Boom! Instant raise!

One thing to keep in mind here is that if you use the range method, the new employer will always give you an offer at the bottom of your range. So, make sure that the bottom is actually where you are comfortable being at. Are there other methods that work better than this? Perhaps, but this method always worked well for me.

Let's talk about option 3 above. You can make extra money for investments and to get out of debt by either getting a second job or by doing some sort of side hustle. I've done both, so I can accurately speak about both options.

When I was in the Navy and had just gotten married, my wife was going to school and working full time. With my E3 pay in the Navy, we couldn't make ends meet on my salary and housing allowance alone, not in San Diego anyway. My wife needed to work, too.

I should have seen this as a red flag at the time, but at one point she asked if she could quit her job and focus on going to school full-time. This became her modus operandi later in the marriage. The only way for this to work was for me to get a second job. Being the blue-pilled simp I was at the time, I decided I was going to be a real man and do that for her.

If you don't know what I mean by blue-pilled simp, I essentially mean a guy who puts a woman on a pedestal and will do anything for her. Blue-pilled is a guy who believes in the idealistic concept of love and commitment, as opposed to the red-pilled pragmatic understanding of intersexual dynamics. Simp is also an acronym that stands for Sucker Idolizing Mediocre Pussy.

A few of my shipmates were moonlighting as security guards for a company in San Diego, and they told me they were always hiring. So, I went to the security company offices with my friends one day to fill out an application and to take my California Guard Card test. The test was easy, and I soon had a second job.

Let me tell you, if you ever want to do a second job, being a security guard is the best. You literally don't do anything. You walk around once an hour, and write in a log book. That is it. If a crime is happening, you are a professional witness. You are not to arrest people. If anything bad happens, you simply call 911, write in your log book what happened, call property management, and collect a paycheck. It really doesn't get easier.

The only reason I stopped doing it was that it really cut into my sleep time working until 1am, then having to get up at 5am to get back to my ship for muster. I started oversleeping and getting to muster late in the morning, and that doesn't go over well in the Navy. I eventually had to tell my wife that I couldn't do it anymore and she needed to get a job again.

I think a better option is the side hustle option. You can do this in various ways. If you don't have any skills, you can do something like Doordash or UberEats to deliver food in your spare time. If you have a nice car, you can offer rides with a company like Lyft or Uber and drive people around in your spare time. In fact, doing these jobs you can probably make just as much as getting a security job, and you can set your own hours.

A side hustle I had when I first got into information technology was to do home computer repair. I would only charge $50 an hour and post ads on Craigslist. It kept me busy enough and I made way more doing that than I did as a security guard. I could have made even more if I put more into it, but I was really only doing it for a little extra hobby cash and to get more computer experience.

There are also online job sites like Fiverr or UpWork where you can do freelance work in your spare time from home. Your options are quite limitless with this if you have marketable skills.

So now that you know the basics about how investments work with compound interest, and you know how to potentially increase your income, let's get into these baby steps shall we?

$1,000 emergency fund

The concept in this baby step is very simple: a lot of our emergencies tend to not really be emergencies at all if we have money available to deal with them. Most people don't do this. What they end up doing if they have some kind of unexpected expense is to put it on their credit card, then the next thing they know, they are in debt for $10,000 to $20,000 and the interest is crushing their hopes and dreams.

To avoid this, start off with a simple $1,000 emergency fund. If you're an 18 year old, this might seem like a lot. If you're an adult living paycheck to paycheck, this also might seem like a lot. It's paramount that you do this, though.

If you're a teenager, you most likely don't have a lot of bills right now. You can easily build up an emergency fund with your part time job. Just be sure to pay yourself first when you get your paycheck. When you hear rich people say that, what they are really saying is paying your *FUTURE* self first by putting your money into savings or an investment.

I recommend taking 10-15% of your paycheck and socking it into a savings account. So if your paycheck is $400, you'd put in $40-$60 into your savings. An even better idea is to ask your company's payroll department to automatically deposit the first 10-15% into your savings account so you don't have to think about it. The rest of the money you can use for whatever teenager things you want! You won't even miss that money, but you'll be glad you have that in an emergency.

Let's say you put the full 15% in your savings, and let's say it was only $60. You'd have your emergency fund fully funded in about 17 paychecks. You can knock out this baby step in less than a year!

For you adults out there, you are probably making more than $400 every two weeks, but the principal is basically the same. You will put 10-15% out of your paycheck into an emergency fund. Let's say you only make $30K a year after taxes. That's roughly $1,153.84 every two weeks. Let's also say you are motivated, and you put in the full 15% into your emergency fund. That would be a contribution of about $173 every two weeks. You will fully fund your emergency fund in only 6 paychecks!

If you think saving $173 will be difficult, you really need to look at what you're spending your money on currently. Are you going to Starbucks every day? Do you eat out for lunch during work? Do you buy DoorDash all the time? All of that can be cut out! You can save so much more by buying your food from the grocery store and making your own food. If you really wanted to get serious about this, you could live off of canned tuna, ramen and cereal for two months until your emergency fund is fully funded. You have to ask yourself how bad you want it, though.

One big difference between what I am telling a teenager, and an adult is where to put their money. This is something I came up with a few years ago, and Dave Ramsey doesn't agree with it although I think he doesn't agree with it because he doesn't quite understand the concept of it.

What I recommend for adults is to open an **Acorns** account. Acorns is an investment account where you put money in, and you can set it to round up all of your purchases to the next dollar and invest that difference into an investment portfolio. So if you buy something at the store for $5.25, Acorns will round that up to $6.00 and transfer $0.75 to your investment account.

What you can **ALSO** do with Acorns is make regular deposits, just like a savings account, but this has a few advantages over a regular savings account that I don't think Dave Ramsey has ever considered:

1. Because it's an investment account, the rate of return is greater than a savings account.
   - A savings account won't keep up with inflation, so by keeping your money in a savings account, you are actually losing money over time.
2. It takes a few days to withdraw this money, so you are less likely to use it for frivolous spending.
   - This is where having a credit card is handy, but you have to be smart with it.

You can sign up for an Acorns account by browsing **http://acorns.comeonmanpod.com** and then both of us will get $5 invested into our accounts! Plus, if you invite friends, you can get the same thing. Everybody wins!

This next part is another area where Dave Ramsey and I differ. He is absolutely opposed to having a credit card, and for good reason. Most people can't handle them. Most people mindlessly rack up large balances and don't realize it until it's too late. If you are that kind of person, then just use a savings account. If you're disciplined and smart, though, then by all means use my method.

What you want to do is get a credit card that has rewards. I personally have an American Airlines card, but there are many others out there. Every purchase racks up air miles or points of some kind. THIS WILL BE USED FOR EMERGENCIES ONLY.

Let's say you have the sidewall on one of your tires blown out, and now you have an unexpected expense of buying a new tire. What you will do is pay for that tire with your credit card, then whatever the amount is, you will withdraw from your Acorns account. It takes about 6 days to transfer those funds. It seems like a lot of time, but it's not enough for the credit card company to charge you interest. Once you get the money deposited in your bank account from Acorns, you immediately pay off your credit card and keep it at a zero balance. You have taken care of your emergency and earned free airline miles or rewards points at the same time! You also are not in debt. Another everyone wins scenario.

Another cool thing about this plan is that you will also be building up a good credit score with this method. Dave Ramsey doesn't think credit scores are that important, but they really are if you are trying to get a loan for something important like a house. The better the credit score, the easier it is to get a loan and have that loan be a low interest loan.

The fun part about this plan is that after a few years, you can get free plane tickets to Hawaii or something else fun. Yes, free! You worked the points system. Most people aren't smart or disciplined enough to do that, and the credit card companies are banking on that.

If you have to dip into your emergency fund, everything else in the baby steps stops, and you return to this step to build that back up. You must always try to keep at least $1,000 in the fund.

The reason I don't recommend the Acorns option for teens is because they can't legally have an investment account at 18. Their parents can open an Acorns Early account for them, but they can't transfer money in and out like they can with a regular Acorns account. I set one up for my daughter, and in the state of Colorado I can't transfer that account to her until she's 21. So it's good as a nest egg account for her, but she can't use it as her emergency fund.

Now that we have our emergency fund taken care of, let's move to the next step.

Pay off debt using a "debt snowball"

If you are reading this book as an 18 year old, then this step may not apply to you just yet. In fact, if you're smart, it will never apply to you. The goal with all of this is to stay out of bad debt. Yes, there is such a thing as good debt and bad debt. Dave Ramsey doesn't really discuss that, but I will.

Bad debt is money you borrow to buy things you don't necessarily need. Or maybe you need it, but you could save up for it or buy something more affordable. Credit card debt and car loans fit in this category. You don't want to be financing your evening at a restaurant or movies after all! When it comes to cars, you don't need the newest and shiniest car to get from point A to point B. In fact, cars are one of the most expensive things you'll ever buy that depreciate over time. If you bought a brand new car, drove it off the lot, pulled a U-turn and tried to trade that car back in, the dealer won't take it back at the price they sold it to you. It immediately loses value as soon as you drive out of the parking lot.

For the most part, if you do the emergency fund step well, you will pretty much never need to use a credit card, and if you are good at saving money, you can buy cars for cash!

Good debt would be a loan for something that appreciates in value over time. A house is an excellent example of this. Dave Ramsey says that a house is the biggest investment most people will make in their lifetime. Robert Kiyosaki, the author of **Rich Dad, Poor Dad** disagrees with this. He says that it's not an investment because it takes money out of your pocket when the house needs maintenance. I tend to agree with Dave on this one. I just bought a house in 2020, and at the time of this writing, it's already appreciated in value by $120,000! I've done a little maintenance on it over the last couple of years, but even with that considered, if I sold it today I'd be making a pretty solid profit.

Another reason why this debt is good is because it basically makes you money out of thin air. This is something else that Robert Kiyosaki talks about in **Rich Dad, Poor Dad**. When you borrow money from a bank, and the thing you buy appreciates in value, you pay the loan back and keep the difference. The difference is money you never had before that was made by borrowing other people's money! The thing here that Kiyosaki recommends though is to use debt like this to buy rental properties for cash flow. I'll talk more about that in the next chapter.

One thing I am thinking of going into debt for at the time of this writing is solar panels for my house. The solar company I talked to will let me finance the purchase, and the payments will be less than what I'm paying right now for my electric bill. On top of that, it will add another 6% value to my house. If my house is currently worth $404,000 according to Zillow, then the panels will add another $24,240 to the sale price. Not to mention the cost savings over the time of the loan will be around $13,500 and there is a huge tax incentive. With all of that combined, I can pay off that loan and still come out on top about $6,000.

All of this being said, there is a reason Dave Ramsey doesn't recommend getting into debt. Most people can't handle it, and don't do it smartly. There's also this mental checkout when it comes to using your credit card or having something financed. You get instant gratification, and the pain doesn't hit you until you've racked up thousands of dollars in debt, and you now have a hard time paying bills and making ends meet.

If you ever find yourself in this situation, you can get out of debt using this debt snowball method. It's pretty simple:

1. Line up your debts in order from the least amount owed to the most owed.
2. Start paying extra money on your least amount owed debt.
3. Pay the minimum amount owed on your other debts.
4. Once your least amount owed debt is paid off, take the money you were paying on that debt including the extra and pay that towards the next least amount owed debt on top of the minimum you were already paying on it.
5. Once that debt is paid off, you do the same thing to the next debt and the next one until they are all paid off.

That sounds all well and good, but what if you can't pay extra on your debts? Go back and refer to the first part of this chapter where I talked about making extra money with side hustles. Dave Ramsey recommends delivering pizzas in the evening and reducing your spending while doing this by eating cheap things like ramen or beans and rice so you can afford the extra money to pay towards your debts. The fact is, if you are motivated enough, you'll do it.

I personally racked up a lot of debt after my divorce, and before I discovered this. I let my ex-wife take pretty much all of our old furniture, and I had to furnish my home from scratch. I also had student loans to pay off. I managed to get completely out from under all of that debt using this method in the span of 5 years. Now the only debt I have is my mortgage, which like I said before is considered good debt.

Increase your emergency fund to 6 months' worth of savings

If you are reading this as an 18 year old, you've probably never experienced this situation I'm about to describe, but perhaps your parents have. This is a very common occurrence for adults. They are so dependent on income from their jobs that even if they hate those jobs, they have to stay because they can't live without that check.

Or, perhaps a recession occurs and they get laid off. When that happens it's panic time. People literally kill themselves over situations like this. Families split up over situations like this. This step will prevent all of that from happening.

Much like your $1,000 in your emergency fund keeps small issues from being true monetary emergencies, having enough in savings to sustain you for six months will keep things like asshole bosses and layoffs from being something to worry about ever again. A radio show host I used to listen to back in the day named Tom Leykis called it *Fuck You Money*. It's enough money in the bank that if your boss pisses you off, you can literally tell him *Fuck You* and walk.

Many bosses would be absolutely shocked by that, for good reason. Most people don't have that kind of money on hand. Most people are easily controlled by their employer this way. This little nest egg will give you an unbelievable sense of freedom. Not to mention, most people have enough self-control not to talk to bosses like that.

I don't personally recommend telling your boss *Fuck You* if you ever do want to quit. I don't believe in burning bridges with employers, and you might want a good recommendation someday. This gives you something to think about though. I recommend at least giving your standard two-weeks' notice at all times unless your boss is just a complete dickhead and deserves being told off.

By now you should have a good idea of what your monthly budget is after creating your initial $1,000 emergency fund and paying off all your bills and getting out of debt with the debt snowball method. This is important because you are going to take your monthly expenses and multiply them by 6 to get how much it costs to live for the next six months without any income.

Before I continue, it's also good to point out that it doesn't take most people six months to find another job. It's never taken me more than a couple of weeks. This is especially true if you don't dilly-dick around and spend all day on the couch watching soap operas and smoking weed just hoping an employer breaks into your house and offers you a job.

No, if you ever find yourself out of work, it's not smart to blow your 6 months of savings taking a mini retirement. This is an emergency fund after all, not a fuck around for 6 months and panic fund. You need to find another source of income as quickly as possible.

You will need to get your resume up to date and start applying for new jobs as soon as humanly possible. The last time I was let go, it was on a Friday. I spent Saturday and Sunday getting my resume up to date and looking for jobs online. I spent the entire next week applying for jobs and doing phone interviews. The second week was spent doing in-person interviews. By the end of week two, I had several offers lined up. If I can do it, you can do it.

Back to the emergency fund. You know all of that extra money you were snowballing into your debts that you finally paid-off? Guess where you're going to start putting that cash now? Correct, you are going to start taking all of that extra money that you no longer have to pay on debts, and you are going to start socking it away in your emergency fund account. You will do this until you've hit your six months of expenses goal.

You'll find that your snowball is pretty big by this point. In fact, you will be shocked how much extra money you have when you don't have any outstanding debt. That means that you will be able to fund your six months savings relatively quickly.

Now we get into the fun stuff...

Invest 15% for retirement

Before we get too far along here, I want to say that if you can, you should definitely invest more than 15%. That is not attainable for a lot of people, but it's certainly something to strive for as you start making more money later on in life. 15% is the perfect starting point, though, and you'll find that you won't even miss it.

I also want to put out there that this is not to be considered financial advice. Please do your own research. I will give you a few methods I'm aware of for allocating your investments, but you will have to pick which one you want to go with. I personally use the Dave Ramsey method because of its simplicity. The only thing I do differently from his is I rebalance my funds once a year based on Tony Robbins' recommendation. I've never had an issue with this method.

Rebalancing investment funds refers to the process of adjusting the asset allocation within a portfolio to bring it back to its original or desired target allocation. Over time, the value of different assets in a portfolio may fluctuate, causing the initial asset mix to deviate. Rebalancing involves buying or selling assets to realign the portfolio with its intended proportions. This proactive approach aims to manage risk and maintain the desired risk-return profile.

For example, if a portfolio initially consisted of 60% stocks and 40% bonds, but due to market movements, the stock allocation increased to 70%, rebalancing would involve selling some stocks and buying bonds to restore the 60/40 balance. By regularly rebalancing, investors can ensure that their portfolio remains in line with their investment objectives and risk tolerance.

Before we get into allocations, let's look at the two vehicles you should be putting your money into. The first one is a Roth Individual Retirement Account (IRA). According to **Investopedia**, a Roth IRA is...

> ...a special type of tax-advantaged IRA to which you can contribute after-tax dollars.
>
> The primary benefit of a Roth IRA is that your contributions and the earnings on those contributions can grow tax-free and be withdrawn tax-free after age 59½, assuming that the account has been open for at least five years. In other words, you pay taxes on money going into your Roth IRA, and then all future withdrawals are tax-free.

The money you put in is money you make after taxes, or your net income. If you didn't know, your employer takes a little bit of money out of your paycheck to pay towards things like taxes, social security, insurance and your 401K. The rest is what is known as your *net income*. The money you make before those deductions is what is known as your *gross income*.

So what does this mean? It means that the money you put into your Roth IRA has already been taxed and can't be taxed again. It's one of the coolest vehicles out there because it grows TAX FREE your entire life, and when you draw on it you don't get taxed either. It's all yours. You get to keep it all.

The drawbacks with Roth IRA's are that you are severely limited as to how much you can contribute. You are only able to contribute up to $6,000 per year until you are 50 years old. After 50 you can contribute up to $7,000. It's not a lot of money if you think about it. $6,000 is only $500 per month. The other drawback is that nobody else is contributing to it. It's your money and yours alone.

That brings us to our second avenue of investment, your 401(k). According to **Nerdwallet**:

> *A 401(k) is a retirement savings and investing plan that employers offer. A 401(k) plan gives employees a tax break on money they contribute. Contributions are automatically withdrawn from employee paychecks and invested in funds of the employee's choosing (from a list of available offerings). 401(k)s have an annual contribution limit of $20,500 in 2022 ($27,000 for those age 50 or older) and $22,500 in 2023.*

One of the differences between a 401(k) and a Roth IRA is that the money you contribute comes out of your gross income. It's pre-taxed dollars. You also have a much larger contribution amount, and bigger companies usually offer some form of contribution match. That contribution match means that your employer is matching the amount of money you are investing up to a certain amount. It's basically free money.

Like I mentioned above, this money comes out before taxes. That means that the government will start taxing your payouts from this fund once you start drawing on it in retirement.

So it's pretty easy to know the difference between a 401(k) and a Roth IRA. One you get taxed on now, the other you get taxed on later.

One thing to consider is that taxes are among the biggest expenses people pay. The rich are always looking for ways to reduce the amount they have to pay to Uncle Sam. So consider this if you are wondering if you should allocate more to your 401(k) or not. Would you rather reduce your taxable income by paying your future self, or would you rather give that money to Uncle Sam where he will inevitably waste it? I personally would rather pay my future self by maxing out my 401(k) and reducing my taxable income than to hand it over to Uncle Sam.

You can reduce your taxable income even further by also investing in a Traditional IRA. A traditional IRA is essentially the same as a 401(k) except it's done individually, and you won't get any company matched "free money" to go with it. You deduct the taxes on the backend when you file your tax return, so the money you are putting in is coming out of your net income in the beginning. Yes, you can have both a 401(k) AND a Traditional IRA at the same time.

A Traditional IRA is just another investment option, but I want you to focus on the Roth IRA and 401(k) initially. Once you have both of these maxed out, if you have money left over, then you should consider opening a Traditional IRA as well.

So which one should you be investing in? I say you should be investing in both up to at least 15% of your annual salary. More if you can afford it. I will also say that since a 401(k) gives you a bigger limit of investment than the Roth IRA annually: $22,500 per year starting in 2023 for a 401(k) vs $6,000 for a Roth IRA. Plus, you are getting free money from your employer if they are offering a company match benefit, so you should at least be starting with the 401(k).

As you start making more money in your career down the road, you will want to eventually max out your contribution to your 401(k), start investing in a Roth IRA, and eventually max that out too. If you do that, you will be doing better than approximately 70% of Americans out there.

If you start doing this at 18, like I showed at the beginning of this chapter, you will easily have over $1 million by retirement.

A lot of people understand the idea of a 401(k) or a Roth IRA, but they have no idea how to allocate their funds. Most IRA's and 401(k)'s offers some kind of automated retirement fund to sock your money into. It's based on your retirement age. For the most part, these funds are trash. They are mutual funds that have a lot of taxes and fees on the back end, and if you look at them over a period of 10 years, they do not beat the market.

One of the things I learned from Tony Robbins is that Index Funds are better than mutual funds. What's an Index Fund you ask? According to **Investopedia**:

> *An index fund is a type of mutual fund or exchange-traded fund (ETF) with a portfolio constructed to match or track the components of a financial market index, such as the Standard & Poor's 500 Index (S&P 500). An index mutual fund is said to provide broad market exposure, low operating expenses, and low portfolio turnover. These funds follow their benchmark index regardless of the state of the markets.*

Basically, an Index Fund will buy up equal parts of stock from the top performers of a particular Index and will park that money. Since there are a lot less trades on the backend, there's a lot less overhead to manage these funds. That means less taxes and fees on the backend.

Index Funds have been proven to outperform regular mutual funds over time because the fund managers aren't trying to guess, gamble and trade their way to better performance. A practice that fails more times than it doesn't.

I mentioned before that you should look at these funds over a period of time to see how they perform. You will hear time and again that past performance is no guarantee of future results. While that may be true, it's the only indicator of potential success we have available. The greater the time span, the better your odds. You see, any investment takes a little bit of risk, but looking at factors such as long-term performance helps you take a more calculated risk.

Another thing you should look at are the prices on the backend. A lot of people don't realize how much money they are actually losing from taxes and fees that are being taken out on the backend. Oftentimes, the returns you are seeing are being reported before the taxes and fees are even taken out. So you want to keep those as low as possible.

Here's an example of a comparison of several large cap Index Funds. I always pay more attention to the 10-year column. If a fund hasn't been around for at least 10 years, I don't put my money into it.

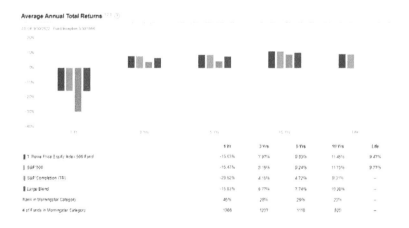

	1 Yr	3 Yrs	5 Yrs	10 Yrs	Life
T. Rowe Price Equity Index 500 Fund	-15.63%	7.97%	8.83%	11.46%	9.47%
S&P 500	-15.47%	8.16%	9.24%	11.70%	9.77%
S&P Completion (TR)	-29.52%	4.15%	4.72%	9.31%	--
Large Blend	-15.83%	6.77%	7.74%	10.28%	--
Rank in Morningstar Category	46%	28%	28%	29%	--
# of Funds in Morningstar Category	1366	1237	1118	820	--

As a personal rule of thumb, I want a 10-year return to beat inflation. At the time of this writing, the current reported inflation rate is a little over 8%. As you can see in the chart above, the 10-year return rate is better than that.

The reason you want to beat inflation is because if you don't, you're actually losing money because the value of your dollars in savings isn't keeping up with the value of dollars in the real world. This is one of the reasons I am very much against saving your money in a standard savings account or even a cash deposit (CD). Usually, the rate of return on those is less than 2%. Well below inflation.

Here's an example of some fees over time reported on an international Index Fund:

Price History By Month ⑦

Actual Values: Sep. 2022 to Sep. 2021

	Close	Low	High
Sep	$14.39	$14.32	$16.23
Aug	$15.84	$15.84	$16.86
Jul	$16.56	$15.28	$16.56
Jun	$15.92	$15.71	$17.55
May	$17.45	$16.04	$17.45
Apr	$17.18	$16.96	$18.80
Mar	$18.53	$17.00	$18.81
Feb	$18.60	$18.37	$19.66
Jan	$19.22	$18.74	$20.25
Dec	$20.15	$19.71	$22.26
Nov	$21.50	$21.50	$22.94
Oct	$22.38	$21.37	$22.57
Sep	$21.57	$21.55	$22.86

I personally like to compare the numbers in the high column with the fees in a few other funds before making my investment choice. You can take an average of all the numbers in the high column to make it simple and compare it with the average in other funds. The lower the cost, the better.

There are probably many more intricate ways to compare funds that a financial advisor would know about, but this is a simple rule of thumb that has worked for me. If you want to get really granular, I definitely recommend hiring a fiduciary over a typical financial advisor or planner. The reason being is that a fiduciary is legally and ethically bound to make decisions in your best interest. Not all financial planners and advisors will do that. Make sure you are hiring a fiduciary.

Now that you have an idea of how to compare funds, let's talk about allocations. Have you ever heard of diversification? Basically, you don't want to put all of your eggs in one basket because if something happens to that basket, you will lose all of your eggs.

The cool thing about Index Funds and Mutual Funds is that they are diversified already by design. You are already investing in many different companies at once when you invest in a particular fund. The thing is some funds perform better than others in any given year. Because of that, you want to put your money in several funds to hedge your investments and keep your overall portfolio growing year after year. There are several ways to do this that I've seen.

The first method is the method that I learned from Dave Ramsey and is very simple. You allocate 25% in Large Cap funds, 25% in Mid Cap funds, 25% in Small Cap funds and 25% in international funds. It looks like this:

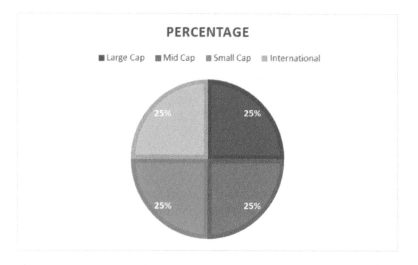

This method is almost all stocks, and some consider it to be rather risky because there aren't too many bonds planned into it. If you look at your individual funds though, sometimes they have things like bonds and commodities included, so I have never sweated it. I'd say this is more of a moderate way to allocate your investments.

The second method I learned from Tony Robbins and Ray Dalio is called the *All Weather* portfolio. It's a little more intricate and is a little harder to figure out percentages based on the typical funds available in your Roth IRA or 401(k) accounts, mainly because a lot of these types of specific funds aren't available in your Roth IRA or 401(k). For instance, I've never seen a 100% commodity fund.

Still though, tho All Weather method of allocation has a proven track record. It's split up by 40% Long Term Treasury Bonds, 30% US. Stocks, 15% Intermediate-Term Treasury Bonds, 7.5% Precious Metals, and 7.5% other commodities such as oil, corn etc. Here is a visual of what it looks like.

PERCENTAGE

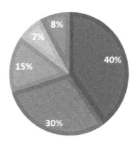

- Long Term Treasury Bonds
- U.S. Stocks
- Intermediate-Term Treasury Bonds
- Precious Metals
- Other Commodities

The idea of the All-Weather method is that stocks are the riskiest, bonds manage that risk, and commodities provide stability. It's designed for risk averse investors, but here's the thing you need to consider: If you are young, you can handle more risk. The more risk, the more reward. I would only recommend this kind of allocation when you are older and closer to retirement.

This last allocation method is how my Acorns account has its aggressive portfolio setup. Again, the more aggressive the portfolio, the more risk, but the greater the potential for reward. Like the Dave Ramsey method, it's split into the same four classifications of Large Cap, Mid Cap, Small Cap and International funds, but the percentages are what makes it more aggressive.

Acorns splits the funds up between 55% Large Cap, 10% Mid Cap, 5% Small Cap and 30% International. It looks like this:

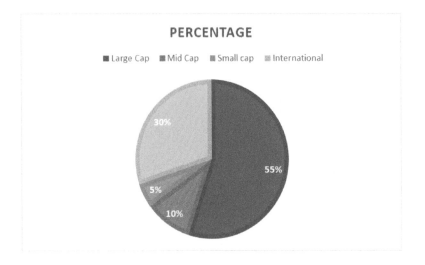

PERCENTAGE

■ Large Cap   ■ Mid Cap   ■ Small cap   ▨ International

Regardless of which allocation method you choose, I highly recommend you pick one and stick with it for several years. Some years perform well, while others perform like trash.

For instance, when Donald Trump was President, I had a year that my 401(k) performed at a rate of return of 22%! That's ridiculously good! Meanwhile, at the time of this writing under Joe Biden, my annual rate of return on my 401(k) has been a God awful -16%. I'm not trying to get political here, but money talks and bullshit walks.

If I were to measure the overall performance of how I allocated my funds based on this year alone, my instinct would be to change things up. You want to look at the performance over a long period of time, just like the stock market. If you look at my overall performance over the last 5 years I've averaged a growth rate of over 20%. Keep in mind that this isn't just rate of return. It's also because I keep contributing.

Another thing you want to do regardless of which allocation method you choose is to rebalance your funds every year. Why rebalance, and what does it mean to rebalance, you ask? According to **Investopedia**:

When you first construct a portfolio, the assets are balanced according to your investment objectives, risk tolerance, and time horizon. However, that balance, known as weighting, will likely change over time depending on how each segment performs. If one segment grows at a faster rate than the others, then your portfolio will eventually become overweighted in that area and may no longer fit your objectives.

Rebalancing the portfolio avoids this overweighting, preserving your desired weighting over time. It is an important step to examine your portfolio annually—by yourself or with your financial advisor—to determine what, if anything, needs to be rebalanced going forward into the next year. Depending on market volatility, you may need to rebalance more often than once a year.

Most investment companies allow you to automate this, so you don't have to think about it. In fact, investing into your 401(k) and/or your Roth IRA really should be fully automated, so you don't have to think about it. I recommend just setting your account to rebalance once a year and don't think about it too much. If you spend too much time thinking about this stuff, you risk analysis paralysis. You don't want that. You'll be fine. Don't overthink it.

Speaking of overthinking, another thing I want you to consider with these investments is to not to get too caught up in what the stock market is doing. For instance, I mentioned above that one year under Trump I had a return of 22%, but this year is -16%. A lot of people panic when the stock market corrects itself, and they pull their money out. This can be a huge mistake.

I had an ex-girlfriend who told me her parents freaked out in the 2000 stock market crash and pulled out all of their 401(k) savings. They now have no money for retirement. When you pull your money out during a correction like that, you basically lock in your losses.

You have to change your mindset about corrections. The best way to look at a correction is that everything is now on sale. For the same amount of money you were investing before, you can now buy more stock! When the stock market comes back up as it inevitably does, more buying means you now will have far more assets than you otherwise would have!

The key here is to do what is called dollar cost averaging. Essentially no matter what the market is doing, you put the same amount of money in every month. This way you buy more shares when the market is low, and over a long period of time you end up with a better overall price for all of your holdings than you would if you would try to time the market.

If you're still a little scared of stock market crashes, consider this from *officialdata.org*:

> *If you invested $100 in the S&P 500 at the beginning of 1930, you would have about $518,989.77 at the end of 2022, assuming you reinvested all dividends. This is a return on investment of $518,889.77, or 9.66% per year.*

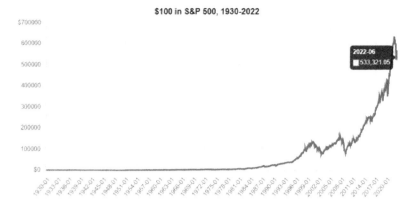

$100 in S&P 500, 1930-2022

Basically, a simple investment of $100 right after the great stock market crash of 1929 would make you a decent chunk of change if you just leave it alone because the stock market has always gone up. Can you imagine how much you would have if you kept investing $100 every month since then? Think about that for a bit.

This investment strategy is a long game. If you are trying to make money quickly in the stock market, I personally think you're better off taking a trip to Vegas. Both are gambling at the end of the day. It's one of the reasons some have called this the slow lane to riches. It takes time, but it has a proven track record of success in the long run

Pay off your home early

There's some disagreement in the financial community about whether or not your home is an asset or a liability. Robert Kiyosaki, the author of **Rich Dad, Poor Dad**, says that your home is a liability because it takes money out of your pocket. If anything breaks, you're on the hook for it. Dave Ramsey on the other hand, says that your home is one of the biggest investments/assets you'll ever make/own. I tend to agree with Dave on this one.

If you buy a home, it's one of the few things that will go up in value. Land is something that they aren't making any more of, after all. Sure, there will be market bubbles and corrections when it comes to real estate, but in the long run the housing market always goes up. Much like the stock market in that regard. This big difference is that the real estate market tends to go up at a much quicker pace.

For instance, I bought by current home in 2020 for about $290,000. When I look on Zillow today, the house is estimated at around $418,000. If I sold it now, that's a profit of $128,000. You can't tell me that's not an asset.

On top of that, since I'm a U.S. Navy Veteran, I was able to buy my home with a V.A. loan. That means that I didn't have to put any money out of pocket down on the loan. Because nothing came out of my pocket on the front end, that means that $128,000 is pretty much free money printed out of thin air. Again, you can't tell me that my home is not an asset.

All of that being said, we all need a place to live at the end of the day, so at some point you are going to buy a home and not really care what the market is doing. You just need a place to live. Wouldn't it be great if you could live somewhere and not have to pay monthly rent or pay a monthly mortgage payment?

By this point in your debt snowball, you'll realize just how much extra money you have when you aren't paying bills. Can you imagine how much MORE you'll have if you didn't have a house payment too? What would you do with all that extra money? Think about it for a minute.

Before we get into how to pay your house off early, let's talk about the elephant in the room. It's almost incomprehensible to some people that this is even possible. Most of us don't know anyone who has actually paid their house off. On top of that, although a home is one of the biggest investments you'll ever make, it's also one of the most expensive things you'll ever buy. Paying it off seems like some pipe dream that will never actually happen.

What if I were to tell you that it is most certainly possible, and you can do it in less time than your loan is set for. For instance, you can easily pay off a 30 year loan in 20 years. Even less if you are serious about it. For instance, my loan company has an early payoff calculator. If I pay an extra $500 a month directly to my principal, I can pay off my 30 year loan in roughly 19.5 years, make 125 fewer payments and save almost $60,000 in interest!

That last part is pretty important. You know how in the previous section I talked about the power of compound interest already? You can use it to your advantage, but so can banks and lenders. They are charging you money for the money you borrow in the form of interest. So by paying back what you borrowed faster, you can save a ton of money in interest payments.

I had a guy argue with me saying that it's terrible advice to pay $500 a month towards your mortgage principal in order to save $60,000 because if you simply put $500 a month into an IRA with an average rate of return of 7% you'll end up with $234,939.87 according to *investor.gov's* compound interest calculator.

At face value, I can see his point. Here's the thing though, we're already investing in an IRA if you followed the last section. So why not pay off your house too and save $60,000 more?

Going back to the early payoff calculator, the more you pay towards your principal, the less payments you're going to make in the long run and the more you are going to save on interest. The key is to pay extra towards your *principal*. A lot of lenders have this option, while some will actually charge you a penalty for paying off your mortgage early. So definitely check with your lender.

If a lender says they will charge a penalty for paying your home off early, find another lender. If you already have a loan with a lender that charges a penalty, look into getting your house refinanced.

If you've been following all of the previous steps, you should have a decent amount to pay towards your principal. You have all of the money you're saving from your debt snowball minus what you are putting in your 401k and Roth IRA left over. All of that, you are now going to pay extra to your principal.

Find yourself an early payoff calculator online and do the math on this. Figure out how long it will take to pay off your home, and then see where you can cut expenses in other areas to see if you can add more to your extra principal payments. The faster you do this, the more money you no longer have to pay to banks and lenders, and the sooner you can keep more of your hard earned money!

Build wealth and give

By the time you get to this point, you'll pretty much be financially free. Congratulations! It's a really good feeling. Most people never get to this point in their lives. Now the fun begins.

At this point, you'll have your standard investments going on autopilot, but now that you don't have a house payment or any other significant debts, you have more money to invest in other things if you want. You'll also be able to give more.

Now, you might be a stingy person and you don't want to give your hard earned money away. Let me try to change your mind a bit about that.

I'm not going to try to plead to your inner altruist or try to make the moral argument that it's the right thing to do. I'm a capitalist. I think if you want to make money, you should go out and make money. Don't expect a handout.

That being said, there are a few good reasons you might consider giving. The first one is that if you give your money to the right organizations, you can write off the donation on your taxes. This effectively lowers your taxable income. We already talked about lowering your taxable income and the benefits in a previous section. This is another way to do it.

Besides lowering your taxable income and NOT giving that money to the government where it will almost certainly be wasted, you don't know how that money is going to be used if you let Uncle Sam take it. At least by choosing an organization, you know what that money is going to be used for.

Just be sure that whoever you donate to has their 501(c)3 status. If you donate to a political organization or a candidate, those donations are not tax deductible. I don't recommend doing that. Besides, if you donate to a candidate, you will be plagued by robocalls and campaign fundraisers for the rest of your life. It's annoying.

Another reason you might consider donating goes back to The Law of Attraction chapter. A funny thing about money Is that if you hold onto it tightly, you tend to have a hard time attracting more. However, if you are more giving with money, oddly enough the Universe tends to bless you with more! Maybe this is woo woo thinking, but I've experienced it so much in my life that I just can't deny it.

At the end of the day, you can choose to give or not to give. That's up to you and by this point you'll have plenty to at least have the option.

At this point in your financial freedom journey, you should also start thinking about more ways to invest your money to build more wealth. You see, an interesting difference between truly wealthy people and the average wannabe is that truly wealthy people like to acquire assets, not liabilities. They like to buy things that appreciate in value. They don't just buy stuff.

A great book to read on the subject is **The Millionaire Next Door** by Thomas J. Stanley. It was a study of thousands of wealthy individuals around the United States. They found that a majority of wealthy people were very frugal. They didn't buy a bunch of junk. The things they did buy were things that were reliable or could gain value in the future.

There are lots of ways you can invest all of this extra money you now have since you are living within your means and have no outstanding debt. Some of the most lucrative of these, most people will agree on, is real estate. In fact, this is where a lot of people make their money quickly.

Just be sure you know what you're doing. Some people get in over their heads with loans and projects, or the market turns, and they find themselves upside down in a bad loan for a house that was overvalued.

Dave Ramsey himself came up with the baby steps above after making millions in real estate only to find himself in a situation where he had too many outstanding loans, and his lender called in all of his loans at once. It's one of the reasons he is adamantly against borrowing money now.

Another great market to invest in is precious metals. In Robert Kiyosaki's book, **Fake**, he talks about what he refers to as *God's Money*, gold and silver. Since the beginning of time gold and silver have always been worth something because of how scarce it is. On top of that, our monetary system was taken off the gold standard in 1971. Before that, every dollar had to be backed by the equivalent amount of gold in the government's possession. That basically means that our dollars no longer have any intrinsic value. It's what's referred to as fiat currency.

Fiat currency is basically *Monopoly* money at this point and the government can print as much of it as it wants. The problem with that is that the more dollars you flood the market with to chase the same finite amount of goods, the more it causes the perceived value of that dollar to drop. That value drop causes an increase in prices for goods. This process is known as inflation.

Precious metals are often used as a hedge against inflation because they always retain some relatively stable value. One of the reasons for that is that the supply rarely changes, because, like I mentioned, it's scarce.

Another great reason to invest in gold and silver is in the unlikely event of a total collapse of the US dollar. I say it's unlikely because most other world currencies are backed by the US dollar, and I don't think the world will let this happen. That being said, this has happened to other countries in the past. It happened in Germany after World War II. It happened in Argentina in the early 80's. It happened in Zimbabwe in 2008 where they had a 5-billion-dollar bill that was only worth 2.5 US dollars. I think you get the point. If something like that happens in the United States, the men with the gold, silver, and real estate will be kings. Just be sure you have enough guns and ammo to defend it...but I digress.

So fiat currency isn't really worth anything and can be manipulated by governments and banks, but precious metals are more stable. Like metals, cryptocurrency can be another good investment vehicle because, like gold and silver, most coins have scarcity built into their algorithms.

For instance, there is a finite amount of Bitcoin that can be mined. This is controlled by the algorithm. It can't be controlled by any central bank or government like fiat currency is because the ledger keeping track of it is decentralized. There's no way of counterfeiting it or debasing it because of the blockchain ledger that keeps track of every Bitcoin ever mined or traded. These are just a few benefits.

The problem with cryptocurrency arises from all of the lesser-known coins or tokens available. You see a lot of people promoting these. One most recent one was Dogecoin. Most of these are pump and dump scams. If you pay attention long enough, you realize that the entire market tends to rise and fall with the price of Bitcoin at the end of the day. So to me it makes sense making Bitcoin your number one investment vehicle in the cryptocurrency space.

Other than that, you would be smart to stick with the most stable coins in the market. Those have always been Bitcoin, Ethereum and Litecoin in my opinion. Stable is kind of an odd choice in words in this space considering the cryptocurrency market is one of the most volatile markets I've ever seen. More on that in a bit.

At the time of this writing, the top five coins according to *coinmarketcap.com* are:

1. Bitcoin (BTC)
2. Ethereum (ETH)
3. Tether (USDT)
4. BNB (BNB)
5. USD (USDC)

Trust me, by the time you take a look, these will have changed, but Bitcoin and Ethereum will probably still be on top of the list.

Some guys like to try and time the market with crypto, but much like the stock market, that is not a good way to go for most people. It's tantamount to gambling. Especially since the market is so volatile.

Back in December 2017 the price of Bitcoin went up to around $17,760 then plummeted to $3,512 around the same time in 2018. More recently the price went up to $66,953 in November 2021 and has dropped to $17,245 at the time of this writing. Trying to time that is just plain stupid if you ask me.

I had at one point completely written off cryptocurrency because of the volatility of it until I had a conversation with one of the internet's best economists, Aaron Clarey. If you don't know Aaron, he's written tons of excellent books like **Bachelor Pad Economics**, **Enjoy The Decline**, and **Poor Richard's Retirement** to name a few. Anyway, Aaron told me that investing in crypto is fine as long as you dollar cost average it like you are doing with your IRA and 401K. Long story short, you really want to play the long game with crypto. Just buy the same amount every month and don't pay attention to the price.

As you saw with the numbers above, yes Bitcoin crashed in 2017, but went way back up in 2021. It takes a few years with crypto, but it tends to always go back up. When you buy at the dips, that's when you tend to make the most money because you are buying at a discount. Because you can't time it though, just keep putting money in and averaging over time, and you will come out on top.

Like any other investment strategy out there, there will be some risk, and you have to be willing to go to zero with it.

A dirty cousin to cryptocurrency is the NFT market. NFT stands for Non-Fungible Tokens. There are lots of practical uses for an NFT, however I don't recommend investing in ANY NFT's at this stage in the game. Most people selling

NFT's are scammers, and the NFT's they sell you aren't worth anything. In fact, every NFT I've heard of has lost value. Do your own research on this though.

I'd like to conclude by reiterating that this really is one of my favorite subjects as I stated at the beginning of this chapter. Learning how to manage my money has been so freeing to me, you wouldn't believe it until you do it yourself.

I have a coaching client who learned this stuff when he was a teenager, and he's got tons of money now along with a regular job doing network security. I personally wished I knew all of this when I was younger because my life would have changed in so many different ways. Luckily, I learned it when I was young enough to still act on it, and I am teaching both of my kids this strategy so they can get a jump on it.

In fact, I set up an **Acorns Early** account for both of my kids so I can start saving money for them, and my daughter can put 10% in from her part-time job now. When she's 21 I can turn it over to her, and she already has a great nest-egg to start her young life with.

If you are 18 and reading this book, ask your parents to do the same!

PHYSICAL FITNESS AND DIET

It amazes me how many people have no idea how to work out. There are lots of funny internet videos about these people using equipment completely wrong. A lot of those videos are staged, I'm sure, but there really are plenty of people who have no idea how to do basic calisthenics let alone how to use regular gym equipment.

If you are eighteen and reading this book, don't let yourself be one of these people. Fitness is important. It might not seem that important now because you have a high metabolism, and you can eat whatever you want without serious weight-gain, but that won't last forever.

If you are an adult reading this book and you have never learned how to work out, that ends today! There is no excuse for you to not know how to work out. You most likely had a gym class of some sort growing up. You just weren't paying attention. Not knowing how to do basic exercise ends today.

In this chapter, I won't be getting in-depth on lots of different workouts. I will be mainly focused on diet, and I will give you four exercises to get you started. In fact, these really are the only four exercises you need to stay in decent shape. Anything else you want to know, I suggest checking out fitness channels on YouTube, or hiring a personal trainer. I am not a fitness trainer, but I do know how to work out and lose weight. I've done it. I have experience. Let's start there.

Back when I was married, I first gained significant weight when my wife was pregnant with my daughter. We often call this sympathy weight don't we? Our wives are gaining weight because they are "eating for two" and we end up gaining weight with them. This absolutely happened to me. My wife would order a bunch of food because she felt starved, but the baby was taking up so much room that she couldn't eat it all. So I would often eat my meal, then finish off my wife's. It wasn't sympathy weight. It was a lack of self-control.

I gained weight and lost it two or three times during our fourteen-year marriage. When she finally filed for divorce in January of 2014, I think I was the heaviest I had ever been, around 230lbs. Now, I'm only 5'9" tall, so according to the Body Mass Index (BMI) chart, I was considered obese. I definitely looked obese, too.

Like I said though, I would gain and lose that weight multiple times during the marriage. I knew how to do it, the trick was staying consistent. What usually would happen was I would get sick of being overweight, and how I looked in the mirror. I would decide that it was time to lose weight. So I would start working out and watching my diet. I would be very consistent with it for several months and I would lose weight. Then we would go on a family vacation somewhere for a week, and when we were there I would let my wife tell me that I could take a break from working out and dieting, and I could enjoy myself. That one week would turn into several weeks, then several months and eventually I found myself being a fat ass again!

It wasn't until I made the New Year's resolution in 2016 that I finally decided to lose weight for good. I looked back on every time I would lose weight and gain it again, and although I would blame my wife for convincing me to take time off when I would travel, I knew that was just an excuse. I decided to take that time off. She didn't make me do it. It was my fault. I owned it.

I decided that I had to make this commitment to myself that I would at least workout five days a week no matter what. Even if I went on vacation, I would at least do SOMETHING! I would at least go for a run. If I didn't, I knew it was only a matter of time before I fell off the wagon again. Never again!

So that's what I did. I made a habit out of working out at least five days a week. Usually a combination of running and weight training. I would frequently add a sixth day of hiking, but I never look at hiking as a workout. That's just fun for me, but it does burn a lot of calories.

Now working out is great, but there's an expression out there that says you can't out train a bad diet. Another similar one is you can't outrun your fork. They're basically saying the same thing. You can exercise all you want, but if your diet is garbage, you won't get good results.

So let's talk about diet for a minute. The way I lost the weight pretty much every time was by using the calories in/calories out (CICO) method. Essentially you burn more calories than you take in. In my opinion, this by far is the easiest way to diet. The reason is because you can pretty much eat anything you want as long as you account for the calories you eat and stay below your daily limit. The cool thing about doing this is that you eventually start to get an understanding of how many calories are in various foods, and you start to make better nutrition decisions naturally.

For instance, a standard Snickers candy bar has roughly 215 calories in it. A regular apple has between 80-95 calories depending on size. An apple also has pectin in it, which is a natural hunger suppressant. It's also more filling. So even though you may have saved enough calories to enjoy a Snickers bar, you know you will feel hungry again 20 minutes after eating it. Eating the apple will make you feel full longer, plus it has less calories. You will start picking the apple more and more often naturally.

Another interesting thing you'll find when keeping track of your calories is how many calories are in the beverages we drink on a daily basis. A 12oz Coke has 150 calories. A 12oz glass of orange juice, which has a ton of sugar, has roughly 167 calories.

Knowing this makes you not want to drink your calories at all because if you don't, you can save your calories for the foods you like to eat. You can still drink other things besides water if you switch to sugar-free drinks.

One thing to note about sugar-free drinks. Some people will say that some artificial sweeteners cause cancer. In my opinion, studies that show these results are remarkably flawed. So, I invite you to do your own research on this subject. Just know that I regularly enjoy Coke Zero, and other similar drinks guilt-free. In fact, drinking these types of drinks are a great way to curb hunger pangs between meals.

So what's the best way to keep track of your calories? In the early days before smartphones, I used to write my calories down on the back of a business card and just do the math. I would start at 2000 calories and subtract what I was eating throughout the day. This actually worked out okay but wasn't very convenient.

Nowadays, I recommend using two apps together to keep track of the calories you eat as well as the calories you burn during exercise. These apps are MyFitnessPal for calorie counting, and MapMyFitness for keeping track of the calories you burn during exercise. A really cool feature of MyFitnessPal is that it asks you what your goal weight is, what your current weight is, what your age is, and what your fitness level is to calculate how many calories you have to stay under each day to reach your goal weight. A great feature of MapMyFitness is that it integrates directly with MyFitnessPal to automatically account for the calories you burn during exercise.

A fun thing to note, when you are heavy and first starting out, burning more calories in the gym gives you extra calories you can enjoy when eating. It's kind of like a reward, now this goes away once your weight gets down to around the 190-195 lb mark. At least it did for me. I found that no matter how many calories I burned in the gym, if I didn't stay under my initial food calorie limit, I wouldn't lose weight anymore. It was frustrating, but you have to keep your eye on the prize here.

Again, this is the simplest way to lose weight. As long as you burn more calories than you consume, you will lose weight. On the opposite side of the equation, if you want to gain more muscle mass you want to eat more calories than you burn. Just be sure to eat clean, and the key is to eat the same types of foods you would eat when losing weight, just slightly more than usual. You can use MyFitnessPal to keep track of this as well. I won't go into more depth on healthy weight gain though because I notoriously suck at it. I will direct you to YouTube if you want to know more about that.

There are obviously other diets you can do out there. In fact, for the last few years I've been seeing a lot of good results on the keto diet. Keto is short for ketogenic, and it's where you eat more fats, a moderate amount of protein and very limited carbohydrates. In fact, you pretty much want to reduce your carbohydrate intake to 20 grams or less a day.

For you folks that don't know your macronutrients, carbohydrates are foods such as potatoes, rice, bread, cereal, pasta etc. You pretty much cut all of these foods out on keto because your body basically just breaks them down as sugar. Whatever your body doesn't use for fuel, it stores as fat.

On keto, you significantly reduce the amount of carbohydrates you consume so that your body goes into a process known as ketosis. That's when your body starts burning fat as fuel instead of carbohydrates.
I really like this diet because I don't have to be so concerned with keeping track of the foods I eat, and the foods that I do eat keep me feeling full longer. When I was counting calories, I often felt hungry a lot, so I had to drink more water and sugar-free drinks just to get me through the day. I don't experience that so much on keto.

All of that being said, keto most certainly isn't for everyone. That's why I spent most of this chapter talking about CICO instead. Still though, I highly recommend you find a diet that you can stick with. All diets work as long as you're consistent.

Enough about diets. Let's talk about fitness. My favorite form of exercise is running. I feel better when I do it, it reduces stress, and it gives me time to listen to audiobooks and podcasts. That being said, strictly doing cardio isn't a good idea in my opinion because just doing cardio, or just dieting, or a combination of both will make you skinny fat.

What do I mean by skinny fat? You will be relatively thin, but when you take your clothes off you will look like crap. You won't have any muscle definition, and you won't be your most attractive self. You'll be thin, and you will have a little bit of fat on you still. You'll be skinny fat!

No, I recommend adding some kind of weight training to your exercise routine to give you some muscle definition. On top of that, the more muscle you have the easier it is to burn fat. It's just a good idea to do this.

So as I said at the beginning, there are pretty much four exercises you need to stay in decent shape. These are the four exercises used by the U.S. Armed Forces, so if it's good enough for them it's good enough for you. Doing these will exercise your whole body.

We already talked about running, so let's start with that. Running not only gives you a cardiovascular workout which is good for your lungs and heart, it also works out your legs and burns tons of calories. Running isn't for everyone though, so a good alternative would be squats. You can do double leg squats, or single leg squats for more of a challenge. Squats will work your glutes more than running will, too, so keep that in mind.

The next exercise is push-ups. The standard push-up will work your chest, shoulders and triceps. There are variations of push-ups that emphasize certain muscle groups more, but the standard pushup is good enough for most people.

After push-ups we have pull-ups or chin-ups. These exercises will work your lats, back, biceps and rear shoulders. A cool thing about pull-ups/chin-ups, and exercising your lats is this is what will give you the V-Taper look. This look has been an attraction marker that women have looked for in men since the beginning of time.

Pull-ups/chin-ups are usually hard for people to do at first. There are two ways of training yourself to be able to do them. The first is by doing negative resistance training. You do this by standing on a chair or something, grabbing your pull-up/chin-up bar, hopping off the chair while holding yourself in a pull-up or chin-up position for as long as possible then slowly lowering yourself to the floor. The other way is to buy some pull-up assistance bands from Amazon or your local sporting goods store. These are essentially huge rubber bands that make doing pull-ups and chin-ups a little easier until you build up your strength.

Finally we have sit-ups or crunches. These work your abs. Having a six-pack is nice, but just remember that a six-pack really starts in the kitchen. You can do a million of these a day, and if you don't have your diet in check you won't see good results. Still, having a strong core is actually pretty important.

If you don't know how to do these, just like any other type of exercise, you can find example videos for free on YouTube.

Once you figure out how to do these workouts, the next thing you'll want to do is make a routine that you can stick to. Like I said before, I like to work out at least five days a week. That means Monday-Friday, and I let myself relax on the weekends. This kind of break keeps me sane but do whatever you can handle. My current routine looks like this:

Monday	Tuesday	Wednesday	Thursday	Friday
Run 4 Miles	Weights: Chest, triceps and shoulders	Run 4 Miles	Weights: Back, biceps and abs	Run 4 Miles

I periodically change this schedule up. For instance, I might get tired of running so much so I will change Monday, Wednesday, and Friday to a weight training day and maybe I'll do legs on Friday, then run on Tuesdays and Thursdays. Something like that. I highly recommend changing your schedule periodically to keep from being bored, and to keep your body guessing. If your body gets used to something, that's how plateaus tend to happen.

That's all there really is to it. If you can follow this advice, you will be able to lose weight and keep it off. I don't think I can make it any easier. Still though, I highly recommend doing your own research to find a diet that works for you and that you can stick with. The same goes for a workout routine. I mentioned it before, but the key to all of this is staying consistent.

DATING/SPINNING PLATES

I am going to give you fair warning now. This chapter will be a very long chapter. I sat down to write out an outline for this and ended up with about four pages of notes that runs the gamut from attraction, to meeting women, and, eventually, to exclusivity. It is almost everything I've learned over the last four years of study and a shit load of practice. My suggestion for you, the reader, is to not take what's in this chapter as gospel. What I lay out here worked for me, but it may not work well for you. That is fine. I ran into the same thing myself. The most important thing is that you go out and at least try it before dismissing it.

Almost all of this information I learned by reading what I now refer to as my "Holy Trinity" of dating books written by Corey Wayne, Dr. Robert Glover and Christopher Canwell. Check out the recommended reading chapter at the end of the book for more information on those. I wanted to give credit where credit is due here, as well as take a moment to thank these men for where I am today, and for their guidance in better understanding women and becoming a better dater.

What do I mean by dating/spinning plates? I think most people know what dating means, but the concept of spinning plates is not so widely known. Especially for teenagers who may be reading this book, but also for bad daters and serial monogamists.

Spinning plates is simply the idea of dating or hooking up with multiple women non-exclusively. The funny thing is that a majority of women do this naturally, but most guys don't. That's why I often joke that men call it spinning plates, women just call it dating.

A lot of serial monogamists and bad daters usually blow off the idea of spinning plates because they think it's somehow immoral or at the very least difficult to do. The truth is that you don't owe anybody anything if you're not exclusive, and this happens to be the most efficient way to date no matter what your goals are.

The reason spinning plates is so efficient is because it allows you to practice, test for interest and test women's abilities to follow your lead much faster than you can by testing it out on one girl at a time, have it not work out, then having to start all over again with another girl.

It also teaches you to be more emotionally detached during the process and not get so hung up if one girl is texting you back or not. When you are texting, dating and hooking up with three or four other girls, the one girl who drops off doesn't matter so much.

A lot of guys develop what's often referred to as sniper mentality or "oneitis". They focus all of their time and attention on one girl at a time, and when things don't work out, they get emotionally crushed at worst, or extremely frustrated at best. Spinning plates eliminates that issue.

I'm not telling you how to live

I've seen dating and relationship coaches make the mistake of doing this. They try to tell guys that pointless hookups and endlessly spinning plates is somehow empty and not as fulfilling as a relationship. I'm not going to tell you that at all.

Some guys want to spin plates forever. For them it's less of a headache because they don't have to answer to anyone, they get variety, and they get the thrill of the hunt. For those guys, I say more power to you! The stuff in this chapter can help with that.

Some guys want to spin plates until they find the right plate. Their "fine China" as it were. That was always my goal in the dating process because I actually enjoy monogamy. I'm not going to sell you on it though if that's not what you want to do. However, if that's your goal as well, then the stuff in this chapter can help with that too!

At the end of the day, as I've stressed in previous chapters, you have to do what's best for you. You have to be your own mental point of origin.

Not an all-encompassing guide

This book is not a dating book. This is just a chapter in this handbook for your life. I will not be able to go as deep into each of these areas as I would be able to if this book was solely a dating book. Someday I may write one of those, but today is not that day!

In this chapter I will give you tips that guys need to learn about attraction and creating what I refer to as H.E.A.T.: Healthy Emotional Anticipation and Tension. All of these qualities are the required ingredient for building attraction. I will also give you tips on how to meet women, how to carry yourself on dates, how to communicate in an attractive way, and even more valuable information.

If you want more in-depth information on any of these areas, though, I highly recommend reading the books I recommend in my recommended reading chapter at the end of this book or reach out to me at **comeonmanpod.com** and check out my coaching offers.

There is no such thing as 'The One'

This is a really hard pill for most guys to swallow. It makes sense, too, because if you really think about it, men are the ones with a more idealistic view of love and relationships. Women would like you to believe they are, but in reality women have more of an opportunistic view of love and relationships. They really want to join a man's lifestyle, and the man himself tends to be secondary in that decision.

The problem with believing that there is just one right person for us, and that she will magically show herself one day, is that this is one of the biggest self-limiting beliefs you can succumb to. I'm going to get into self-limiting beliefs a little later in this chapter, but for now let me just say it is something you believe in strongly, however instead of propelling you forward it holds you back.

You'll start looking at every woman who has the slightest bit of interest in you as your possible "one" and that will keep you from seeing all of the other potential better options that are available to you. What you'll inevitably do is try to make this girl you think is your soulmate fit into this imaginary mold in your mind. You'll overlook her red flags and try to rationalize to yourself reasons you can work with all of her problems. Meanwhile, much better options around you will go overlooked because you've made your mind up already.

Another problem with it is that it's just completely unrealistic. Roughly eight billion people live on this planet, and roughly half of them are women. What are the odds that of those four billion women, your one true "soulmate" is even in the same state as you, let alone the same city? The odds are astronomical.

Now I hear what you are thinking, "But Paul, if it was meant to be by The Universe, wouldn't The Universe put my soulmate in close proximity?"

That's perhaps the case but let me ask you a question. What happens when some gal shows high interest in you, has an amazing body, and shags like a porn star? You start thinking that she's definitely the one, but here's the rub. She's not. Rather, some other chick on the other side of town, lonely and swiping on a dating app is your mystical soulmate. You will never get a chance to meet her because you believe this girl who just rocked your world is your soulmate, and now you're thinking with your dick. This sort of thing happens all the time.

Guys think they've found their soulmate only to date them for a while and figure out they're not compatible and go through a breakup. Hell, they might even marry this person, go fourteen years like I did and end up divorced, only to try and repeat the process. It's an endless loop of trying to find your REAL soulmate, and when it's all said and done, you've spent your whole life spinning your wheels and have three divorces under your belt.

Perhaps you're more of a numbers guy. I've already said there are roughly four billion women on the planet. Let's just say this girl who just rocked your world in bed is one in a million in your mind. If you divide four billion by one million, that means there are roughly 4000 girls just like her out there. Do you see where I'm going with this?

They say that the definition of insanity is doing the same thing over and over again and expecting different results. Let's just end that right here. There's not just one right girl for you out there. There are many possible good women out there for you. It's your job to sort through them and find the one or ones you like.

To do that, I highly recommend dating multiple women at once. A lot of guys in the men's space refer to this as *spinning plates*. You may also hear it referred to as *plate theory*. What does it mean to spin plates?

Wikipedia defines spinning plates as:

> *Plate spinning is a circus manipulation art where a person spins plates, bowls and other flat objects on poles, without them falling off.*

You've seen this act before right? A guy is holding various poles and has spinning plates at the top. They end up with quite a few going at once. Sometimes the plates fall off and crash, but then the performer just picks up another plate and puts it on the pole. You get the idea.

Well instead of plates, you are doing this with women. Instead of putting them up on a pole, they are riding your dick. You get the idea.

A lot of men think this would be too difficult or just immediately dismiss it for a variety of reasons. A few of those reasons are:

- I don't want her to think I'm a player.
- I'm a one woman man, and I'm loyal.
- It's too hard to deal with one woman, let alone multiple women.
- It's hard enough getting one date, how am I supposed to get multiple?
- What if I get an STD?

So what these men tend to do is date with what's often referred to as "sniper mentality." They set their sights on one girl at a time, much like a sniper does. Guys who do this often find the dating scene very frustrating because they put all their time, energy, and emotions into one girl. When things don't work out, they must start the whole process over again from scratch and it becomes exhausting.

Let me tell you this, the women you are sniper dating are not doing the same. Women are natural plate spinners. In fact, I once had a guy in my TikTok comments say it best, "Men call it spinning plates, women just call it dating." Women always have several male orbiters around them. On dating apps, they have way more options than men do. This puts them in a good position to go on lots of dates to filter out the guys that won't be a good fit for them and spend more time with guys who are a better fit. They do this because they are looking for their very best possible option. They also do this because it's highly efficient. Men need to do the same.

So let's look at some of those objections:

I don't want her to think I'm a player.
You don't want her to think you're a player, but guess why players are so successful? Because they play the game. I'll get into it a little later, but women are more attracted to men with options. Don't apologize for it. Take advantage of it.

I'm a one woman man, and I'm loyal.
When you start dating, that's all it is. Dating. You're not married to her, and she's not married to you. She is going to be dating other guys to weigh her options. You're a fool if you don't do the same. Just remember, you're not exclusive until you have the exclusivity talk, not before then. She knows this and expects you to have that understanding.

It's too hard to deal with one woman, let alone multiple women.
The guys who believe this are typically not that good with women to begin with. If you're a strong masculine man who knows how to lead a relationship, you'll find that women aren't that hard to deal with because they want to follow your lead. On top of that, dealing with multiple women makes the dating process easier because you're less needy. You don't care if one of your "plates" flakes or falls off completely because there's always another plate. It becomes easier to shrug that sort of thing off because you have more options. Not being needy is a quality that women find attractive.

It's hard enough getting one date, how am I supposed to get multiple?
For you guys who think that it's hard enough to get one date, like I said above, and I will say multiple times in this chapter, women find men with options attractive. The late Alan Roger Currie, the author of **Mode One**, said it very simply: pussy attracts pussy. If you can get one girl, it makes it easier to get another one. Now, until you get to that point you can sort

of fake it until you make it. A woman's imagination is your best tool here. More on that later.

What if I get an STD?

Dr. Robert Glover once said the following about guys who are overly concerned with catching an STD:

> In my experience, most men who have an overwhelming fear of STDs usually also have an overwhelming fear of vaginas and the women who own them. The fear of catching something is just a pretext to avoid vaginas.

To ease your fears with this, just know that there are only four STD's that can't be cured, but all of them can be treated. One of those, Human Papillomavirus (HPV) typically clears up on its own over time with men. You just have to worry about warts and getting those things frozen off by a doctor. Women have a bigger issue with HPV, so just be thankful you have all of that male privilege you keep hearing about. For the most part though, as long as you wear latex condoms and get tested regularly, you'll be just fine. Relax.

Hypergamy

Depending on who you are talking to, hypergamy can either be a dirty word or the word that will save you time, money, grief, and heartache. I'm not going to go into depth about it, but it is essential for men to understand what it is and how they can use it to their advantage. A lot of guys hear about hypergamy and think that it's a bad thing and that all women will cheat on them eventually because of what it means. That's not necessarily the case if you work with it.

Essentially, hypergamy is the name we give to female mating strategy. Women are sexually attracted to strong masculine men who are fit, daring, bold, exciting, etc. We call these traits "alpha traits" to keep things simple. Women also want a guy who is a good protector and provider and is generally nurturing. We call these traits "beta traits." Notice I said "also" there. That's because hypergamy is dualistic. I believe it was author Rollo Tomassi who coined the phrase "alpha fucks, beta bucks" to really simplify this.

The thing about hypergamy is that because women want both traits, if the guy they are with doesn't have both, they will absolutely seek what they are missing outside of the relationship. For instance, let's say you are a strapping dude with almost all alpha traits. She'll enthusiastically give you access to all three of her holes for sexual gratification, but when you're done she will look for emotional, and, often, financial support from one of her numerous beta male orbiters who are just waiting for such an opportunity.

Likewise, if you are that guy who makes a lot of money and focuses all of your energy on putting food on the table, being a good listener, doing the dishes, etc. just hoping for a piece of tail, then your primary traits are beta traits. She will seek her exciting alpha needs outside of the relationship with either an exciting, charismatic guy from the sales department, or at the very least from a trashy sex novel. For you, though, she'll have frequent headaches among many other excuses to avoid sex with you.

Because men are so driven by our sexual strategy, which amounts to unlimited access to unlimited sex, there is a huge emphasis on being an "alpha bro" in the men's dating space. There is definitely some merit there, but if your goal is also to have some kind of long term relationship, then you must also possess some of those beta qualities as well.

If your goal is to only hit it and quit it, then you need to maximize your alpha traits. You have to learn what they are, apply them effectively, and make them a part of your default personality. You don't have to worry about the beta traits at all.

The difference between alpha and beta traits can best be explained by the neurochemical response these traits trigger in women. Alpha traits are traits that bring a woman a feeling of physical attraction and excitement. This is driven by *dopamine*. Beta traits make a woman feel comforted and taken care of, and this is driven by *oxytocin*.

The key concept here if you want to use hypergamy to your advantage and get your needs met as well, is to always default to your alpha traits. Whatever your primary traits are, that is how she will see you. You can't act beta 80% of the time and try to sprinkle in some alpha 20% of the time because she will only see you as a beta. This is great if you don't mind her fucking other dudes, but most guys would frown on that.

What women respond to

I first heard this concept from an old clip of a daytime talk show. They had a bunch of pickup artists (PUAs) on the panel, and the host asked what they thought women wanted. Ross Jefferies, the legendary master of using neuro-linguistic programming (NLP) in speed seduction said that he didn't care what women want. The reason being is because there are things women say they want, things they think they want, but the things they respond to are oftentimes very different.

How many times have you heard a woman say that they want to date a nice guy, but every guy they get with is a complete jerk? The fact of the matter is that most women have no idea why they are attracted to the guys they end up with. To them, it's just "something about him." This is also a really great reason why it's a good rule of thumb to never take dating advice about women from women. I could write an entire chapter on that, but I think I'll save that for another book.

So let's start with the fact that, in general, women are security seeking creatures, and they respond to strength. I learned the first part of this concept from Dr. Robert Glover, and the latter from Christopher Canwell. Once you have a good understanding of that, everything else in this section will make sense.

Now a lot of guys hear the security-seeking part and immediately think that women only care about money. That's not necessarily the case. What is more accurate is that women are attracted to the traits a man has that he could use to acquire money, traits like being charismatic, being bold, taking calculated risks, and being assertive and decisive. All of those traits are commonly found in successful men who make good money. Those also happen to be highly attractive qualities to women because it makes them feel safe and secure. Money itself is just a bonus.

Let's take money out of the equation for a minute to illustrate this. Let's say there is some kind of global economic collapse, and overnight the dollars in your wallet are worthless. Everyone is now in fend-for-themselves mode, and society starts to devolve into chaos. Men who are charismatic, bold, assertive, decisive, and take calculated risks will be the kind of guys who get shit done. Their characteristics will offer safety and security to women regardless of money.

Those are characteristics of strength. It also turns out that guys with those types of characteristics are usually the kind of guys that stay in shape, so physical markers of that sort of thing are a small waist, a v-tapered back, and big shoulders. Those characteristics often translate to physical strength. All of these things make women feel safe and secure.

Another characteristic of men who can acquire money and resources that women find attractive is confidence. I wanted to list this one separately because it's such a powerful quality that when properly applied can significantly raise your status in a woman's mind.

Have you ever seen an ugly fat dude with a smoking hot woman and said to yourself, "that dude is punching outside of his weight class." It's the number one reason that the idea of "leagues" is nonsense. A guy who can confidently approach a woman and strike up a conversation regardless of their respective physical attractiveness will give a woman the same psychological tingling feeling that men get when we see a woman's boobs. The reason being is that just like men are hardwired to be attracted to a great set of knockers, women are hardwired to find confidence sexy.

So knowing that women are security-seeking and respond to strength, a great rule of thumb when dealing with women is this: *whenever you're in doubt, think of the strongest action you can take, and do that.* This will set you up for the next concept that I want to tell you about.

Women love to be told no. That's a very simple way of saying that women respond very well to boundaries, and an easy way to display your strength is to tell a woman "no" in order to enforce your boundaries. One of the reasons for this is that almost nobody tells attractive women no. They are very much used to getting their way all of the time because everybody wants to fuck them. So when a guy tells them no and has the strength to set boundaries in the face of her beauty, it really sets him apart. It makes them really stop and think about how you're different from most guys. It's a real turn on for them.

Sure, they may pout and get upset at first, but oftentimes that's a test to see if they can violate your boundaries, to make you back down. Stay strong young man. She wants to know that your strength is real.

Another attractive trait that will demonstrate your strength and leadership is to be assertive and decisive. A guy who doesn't push for what he wants, and, likewise, doesn't even know what he wants is passive, and being passive is a feminine trait. So if you can make decisions quickly, and push for what you want, you are acting in your masculine, and feminine women prefer masculine men.

This was a difficult concept for me to put into practice and took some work. After all, so many things in this life really don't matter. I often will use the classic dinner debate between men and women. You know the one where the guy really doesn't care where they eat, and he's afraid of picking the wrong place, so he asks his wife or girlfriend where she wants to eat. She of course doesn't know, and the mindless, circular conversation continues.

The best way to resolve this kind of a situation is to be assertive and decisive. If you really don't care where you want to eat, then it doesn't matter which place you choose. Just pick a place that sounds good to you and go with it. That is being decisive. In his book, **Think and Grow Rich**, Napoleon Hill says that one of the traits all successful men have is that they make decisions quickly. Be like those men.

You demonstrate assertiveness by telling her where you are taking her to eat as opposed to asking her to join you or asking her if the place you pick sounds good. Just say something like, "Honey, we're going to Applebee's tonight. Wear those new cute shoes you bought." Believe it or not, this sort of thing really gets a woman's panties wet. They don't want to make decisions. They just want to show up looking hot and go along for the ride.

A lot of this comes down to the fact that women really like a man who sets the tone and takes the lead in a relationship. Although you might meet some women who THINK they want to be in control of a relationship, a lot of the time women only think so because none of the guys in their pasts have ever taken the lead. She really doesn't want to be there. It goes against her feminine nature to be in charge.

A lot of guys raised under modern feminism are shocked to hear this. We've been taught our whole lives about equality and how women want to be considered equals to men. However, the divorce rates prove this isn't true at all. We've experimented with this dynamic for the last fifty years or so, and women aren't happier. They really don't want to be in charge, especially not in a relationship. Even the most bossiest of boss babes really wants a guy who is more bossy and can put her in her place.

Like it or not, men and women aren't equals. Our differences are meant to complement each other. A great way to think about this dynamic is to consider how a car has only one steering wheel. Someone needs to drive. As a man, it's your job to drive and lead the interaction.

Besides picking the places to eat, and making decisions like that, you can also lead the interaction by being a gentleman. Do things like open doors for her, hold her hand and lead her through crowded rooms, take her jacket or help her put her jacket on at restaurants. When walking down the street, walk on the street side to position yourself between her and any traffic. Some guys think that doing these things is putting her on a pedestal or acting like a simp. It really isn't. It's all about you setting the tone and taking the lead in a relationship. It shows her that you are in charge.

Another thing that creates H.E.A.T. is by being a bit of a mystery. Women are like detectives in Nancy Drew novels. They want to unravel the mystery that is you. A lot of guys ruin this mystery by wearing their hearts on their sleeves and telling women everything about themselves. The ironic thing about doing that is it makes her lose interest in you quickly. You spoiled the mystery and ruined her fun.

Some great ways to be a mystery is by keeping texting and phone calls to a minimum between dates. In fact, texting and phone calls should be for planning dates only. You get to know a woman in person, on the date itself. This is really hard for a lot of guys in the modern age to understand because they get a dopamine hit from the text interaction. Women do as well, but it's worse for men because we are more physically driven in relationships. We want to fuck her, and you can't fuck her over the phone. You can't even smell her perfume!

She, on the other hand, gets a lot of her emotional needs met with text interactions and lengthy phone call conversations. She is getting her proverbial cup filled, but you aren't. So cut that out and save it for when you're together. On top of the fact that you are often giving too much away in these text and phone conversations, you're not giving her enough time to wonder about what you're up to or who you might be hanging out with. Her wondering is forcing her to think about you, and that all builds anticipation and tension.

Now, I mentioned her wondering about who you might be hanging out with. This is a very important factor that men often overlook. Women are actually more attracted to men who have options with other women. The late Alan Roger Currie, often regarded as the Godfather of Direct Game, said it very simply, "pussy attracts pussy." This is one of the reasons that spinning plates and dating multiple women is actually the most efficient way to date regardless of your goals with women. The more women you date, the more attractive you become.

This comes down to a psychological form of social proof called *pre-selection*. Women throughout history have had to determine the worthiness of a mate by analyzing cues from men's behavior because women experience the greater direct impact and long-term responsibility if they become pregnant. For instance, if a woman becomes pregnant during a random act of sex, her body has to deal with those consequences for nine months afterwards as the baby develops and grows inside of her. A man only has to donate sperm. So from an evolutionary standpoint, women have learned to be choosier by paying close attention to men's status, physical attributes, and behavior and what those characteristics likely telegraph about his fitness as a mate, protector, and provider.

Getting to know a man, testing his strength and really seeing if he's a good quality mate can sometimes takes months or years to fully weed out. Since a woman's value is often derived from her youth and beauty, at least from a reproductive standpoint, she can't afford to waste a lot of time with the mate selection process. At least, they couldn't historically, and that is what has been programmed into their DNA. So a psychological short cut was also programmed-in that concludes that if other women find a guy desirable, he must be good mating material. This is pre-selection, and that's why pussy attracts pussy.

The hard part about getting multiple women for most guys is getting the first one. So how do you get that first one without already having the others? Be a mystery. A woman's imagination can be used to your advantage. If she asks if you are seeing anyone else, keep your answers vague. Say something like, "I always have room for one more" with a smirk and a wink. I learned this from Corey Wayne. This is a playful way of not really saying whether you are or you aren't. Let her hamster wheel grind on that, and while it's grinding, who is she thinking or even obsessing about? Do you see where I'm going here?

Likewise, this is one of the reasons I often tell guys not to take first dates out on a Friday or a Saturday night. Fridays and Saturdays are prime date nights. Guys who have a choice with women always have plans on Fridays or Saturdays. So if this is a first date, and you ask her out on those nights, she KNOWS that you don't have something else going on. This subconsciously can tip her off that you really aren't as desirable by other women. So keep first dates on any other night between Sunday and Thursday.

Also, this means you should not be texting women and using dating apps after about 7pm on Friday or Saturday either. If you are doing that, they also will know that you don't have anything else better going on those nights. If they text you, don't answer until the morning. Let that trusty hamster wheel spin on what or who you might have been doing the night before.

One of the worst things a guy can do that absolutely kills attraction is to tell a girl he just met that he's not seeing anyone else. This basically is a red flag either consciously or subconsciously for women. It tells them that you don't fuck.

Acting in this manner kills two birds with one stone. You are using pre-selection to your advantage, and you are being a mystery. I can't stress enough how being a mystery is essential in the early stages of dealing with a woman. I've learned from Rollo Tomassi in his book, **The Players Handbook**, that women really love nothing better than to feel like they've figured you out using nothing but her feminine intuition. Don't ruin that for her, because she needs that to really invest in you.

Another thing women really respond to positively is a man who is in good control of his emotions. You often hear this referred to as frame control or being in your center. A guy who isn't easily rattled can act quickly and level-headedly in an emergency. I raised my kids since they were little with the mantra of "if you panic, you die." The same can be applied to dealing with women, and how they will test men to make sure they are in control of their emotions.

We often hear these tests referred to as shit tests, strength tests, or fitness tests. They are all the same things. They are what women do to men they have a sexual interest in to make sure he is the strong masculine man they think he is. Dr. Robert Glover says it very well: "Women don't test men to be shitty. They test men to make sure they have their shit together."

A lot of men fail these tests because they think those women are being mean, rude, disrespectful, or are playing games in general. This is the wrong mentality when looking at what motivates these tests. Men should actually learn how to deal with them, and eventually welcome them. Women will only test you if they have a sexual interest in you. She doesn't test the guys she's put in her friend zone, or, if she has tested those guys, they are the ones who failed the test which is why they are in the friend zone.

Now, there is a distinct difference between your typical shit test and a woman just being a bitch. A shit test is usually a playful jab. It's almost like fun, flirty banter, but she'll say something to try to knock you off your center. For instance, if you are a shorter guy, she might say something like "I thought you'd be taller." You see, it's not necessarily that mean, but it's also not a compliment.

An example of her just being a bitch is if you walk up to talk to her and she says, "Ew, get away from me you fat fuck!" See the difference? If a woman says something like this, I'd just chuckle to myself, shake my head and walk away. No need to engage with that sort of behavior. Even in this circumstance, losing your cool is not the right move.

So how do you handle shit tests? There are two ways that I found that worked well for me. There are other ways to be sure, but these can be applied to pretty much any circumstance.

1. Act indifferent
2. Agree and amplify

I like to just keep it to these two because it makes it very simple. Having too many options tends to hinder our ability to think quickly and becomes confusing. So stick to these two, and they will get you through any situation a woman throws your way.

Acting indifferent is pretty straight forward. It's pretty much the example I gave you with the woman acting like a bitch. Shrug off the remark, and act either like she never said it or that it had zero effect on you. For instance, I have a female friend who I often jog with. Sometimes she likes to throw playful barbs at me when we go for a run. Maybe she'll make fun of my hairline or whatever. I just don't react with any kind of emotion or facial expression. I literally shrug it off like it doesn't matter because it doesn't. When she sees that she can't get a rise out of me, she knocks it off. It's a very simple way of dealing with stuff like that.

Agreeing and amplifying requires a little more thought and free association. You have to be quick-witted sometimes to pull these off, so it helps to have a few go-to's you use when you hear the same kind of jabs or shit tests. For instance, if you are a shorter guy and she says the, "I thought you would be taller" line, a good response could be, "Yep, the secret is out. I am in fact a midget!" The idea is to agree with her, yes you are short, then make it more absurd, you're a midget. You agree and amplify. It makes sense, right?

Just to give you a few more you can keep in your back pocket, these responses or variations of these can help:

She says...	Agree & amplify with...
You're bald	Yeah, but it makes me more aerodynamic!
Your car is a rust bucket	It really is, only the paint is keeping it together. I can't wait for my Lambo to get out of the shop!

| I bet you have a really tiny penis | It really is, in fact you'll have to bring a magnifying glass for later to see it. |
| We're not having sex tonight | Of course not, I'm a choir boy |

These are some common shit tests you'll see while dating, but in reality women test men in other ways as well. I'll get into that more in the long-term relationship chapter, but for now just know that women are always going to be testing you, so it's just a safe rule of thumb to assume that everything she is doing is a test. The more you pass her tests, the less she will actually do it, but she will always test on occasion just to keep you on your toes. If you keep your wits about you though, never get complacent, and assume everything is a test, you'll be just fine.

Let's talk about physical attraction for a little bit. A lot of guys think a man has to be 6ft tall to get women. After all, a lot of women put that as a stipulation on dating apps don't they? A lot of guys refer to this as part of the three 6's (Or four 6's depending on who you talk to). The Three/Four 6's are:

- You have to be 6ft tall
- You have to make a 6-figure salary
- You have to have 6 pack abs
- You have to have at least a 6in cock

The fact of the matter is that the average man is only 5ft 9in tall anyway, and women aren't very good at measuring things. Have you ever seen them try to measure something? They don't pull out a tape measure, they hold their hands out the length of something then go to the store and try to use that same hand measurement to figure out what they want. Let's just say, it's less than accurate.

The truth is that women just want a guy who is taller than them most of the time. Having a guy who is taller makes them feel safe and secure. So if you are only 5ft 7in tall like Tom Cruise, don't worry about it so much because there are plenty of women who are only 5ft tall. On top of that I've seen shorter guys get with taller women. Most of the time if you don't make a big deal about it, they won't either. Just remember, we're all the same height when laying down anyway!

Sticking with the Three/Four 6's, you don't have to make a 6-figure salary either. In fact, there are plenty of guys that work in technology that make 6 figures, but they can't pull women. Largely because their social skills suck and they have poor hygiene. It's really not about the money at the end of the day. The average dude in the United States makes somewhere between $30K-$50K a year and does just fine. Women are more concerned with your ability to keep your finances in order and be able to pay your bills. Go back to the chapter on how anyone can get rich.

What about the abs though? You don't really need these either. In fact, roughly 75% of Americans are obese. As long as you're just not fat, you'll already be in the top 25% of men in America. You just need to be in better shape than the guys around you and you will clean up on the dating market.

Ok, so you don't need THOSE 6's, but a woman really does want a guy that has a big dick, right? The truth is, a 6in dick really isn't that big. In fact, it's pretty close to the average which is about 5.16in. There was a massive study that was published in the British Journal of Urology that looked at over 15 thousand penises to come up with that average. It turns out that the vast majority of dicks are within a few centimeters of each other. We've already established that women can't measure that well anyway, so you think they can tell the difference of a couple of centimeters?

In reality, most of this stuff doesn't matter at all because women respond to how you make them feel in the moment. This includes sex as well. If you're seriously lacking in the cock department, then work on your tongue game. Learn to eat pussy really well. That, or you can bring in toys to the bedroom for the assist. Mr. Vibrator on her clitoris while you're getting yours works wonders, and you will still get all of the credit for the interaction.

The last thing I want to talk about as far as what women respond to is body language. A lot of men don't understand the impact that body language plays in attraction. Women naturally pick up on body language easier than men do. In fact, if you play a movie with the sound off and make men and women watch it, a vast majority of women will be able to tell what's going on based purely on the body language alone. A smaller number of men can do the same thing.

As a rule of thumb you want to have relaxed, wide open body language when talking to women. You want to sit with your legs spread open. You want your shoulders back. You want to hold your head up high, and generally be comfortable in your own skin. You also want to take up a lot of space around you. When you greet people, nod your head up. This is very alpha body language.

You want to avoid closed off body language like crossing your arms and tucking your chin. You also want to avoid sitting with your legs crossed close together, because that is a very feminine way to sit. You don't want to nod your head down when you greet people because this is often shown as a sign of submission. If this is a real struggle for you, don't nod at all.

I really want to reiterate here that largely what you are going for in this section is creating H.E.A.T. in a woman. Again, this stands for Healthy Emotional Anticipation & Tension. All of those things are the ingredients necessary to bake a cake of attraction in a woman. If you can master these things in this chapter, you will be in the top percentage of men who really understand what women find attractive, and you can use it to your advantage.

Let go of attachment to outcome

This is going to be the hardest thing for most men to learn how to do. It certainly was for me. You see, we've learned from Buddha thousands of years ago that attachment is the cause of all suffering, yet none of us got the memo on that. I certainly didn't.

We tend to put a lot of attachment on outcomes in all things in life. We want a certain outcome when we apply for a job. We want a certain outcome when we go to the gym. We want a certain outcome when we ask that cute waitress at Waffle House for her number. Then when we don't reach that outcome, oftentimes we're crushed.

You see this play out time and time again on the dating circuit. You see this play out for men right after a breakup, especially. They want to try to recreate something special that they lost so they can get back to some semblance of normalcy and get back to their routine.

Perhaps they were married for 10-15 years and haven't figured out how to be alone. I had one of my 3% Brothers join me for a podcast recording once, and he said it very well about his experience of not feeling comfortable being alone. He said that when he walked around his house when it was just him there, the silence was deafening! So what did he do? He rushed out to try and fill that missing void. He was attached to the idea that he couldn't handle being alone.

That rush into trying to not be alone ended up landing him in a relationship where although the sex was out of this world, the rest of the relationship was toxic as hell. It culminated in him spending the night in jail due to false domestic violence charges, and him eventually kicking her out of his house...at which point he found himself alone again. If you want to hear that full story, visit my YouTube channel and search for "Crazy Girlfriends, and Fake Domestic Abuse Accusations."

Another thing that men tend to do when dating is falling prey to a phenomenon called *Chronesthesia*. This is essentially mental time travel. Guys meet a woman in person, on social media or on a dating app and start chatting with her. Then they mentally time travel to a future with this woman. They imagine what it's like to fuck her, what their house is going to look like, what their kids are going to look like. They start planning out their entire lives with this girl before even having a single date with her. When it doesn't work out that way, she flakes, ghosts, or she goes on that date and it just doesn't work out, it's devastating.

I'm not saying that you shouldn't have goals and work to achieve those goals. Setting goals and working towards them is very important. The problem is attaching yourself mentally to the outcome of those goals. There are a couple of good reasons to avoid this.

One, when you become attached to an outcome, if that outcome doesn't happen the way you expect, you get crushed mentally. This is one of the reasons a lot of guys go MGTOW (Men Going Their Own Way). They are attached to a perfect idealistic life with women, and when that doesn't pan out, they are crushed mentally, decide the juice isn't worth the squeeze, and give up completely.

Another reason is that when you are pushing for a particular outcome, especially when it comes to relationships, you really put off a needy vibe that repels women like water repels cats. Women can smell neediness like sharks smell blood. Evolutionarily speaking it is not in men's nature to want to push for commitment. Men's sexual strategy historically has been to spread our seed far and wide with as many sexual partners as possible. It was women who were trying to lock down a man for protection and provisioning. So when you are pushing for a particular outcome with relationships and dating, you are essentially acting like a woman which is ultimately unattractive to women.

Let's revisit getting crushed mentally when things don't go as expected. This actually holds a lot of people back because if things don't go exactly according to plan, it often puts them in a downward spiral. If you go back to my Law of Attraction chapter, you know that this sort of negative thinking will cause more negativity to show up in your life. You'll keep having dates or relationships fail because that becomes what you are focusing on the most. You stop focusing on what you DO want, and really start focusing on what you DON'T want.

So what's the solution for this? Take a deep breath, become aware of your attachment to a particular outcome, and let it go. That's certainly one way of doing it, but I'll tell you what really helped me let go of that attachment, especially when it came to dating.

I started treating dating like a science experiment. I learned this concept from Dr. Robert Glover, but it really became a game changer for me. Think for a minute about what scientists are doing when they create an experiment. They create a hypothesis; they test that hypothesis; and if it can't be disproven, they raise it to a theory, right? We call this the scientific method.

There is no expectation or attachment to outcome with the scientific method. You are simply collecting data. So when you apply this to dating, you will do the same thing. You are not trying to push for sex on a first date. You are not trying to get a girlfriend. You are simply taking advice and applying it in a social situation to see what works and what doesn't. You are testing a hypothesis.

If something you test works well for you, great! Keep doing that on future experiments (dates). If something you test doesn't work well for you, great! Discard it and try something different. Eventually you will find a formula that works well for you consistently, and, even better, what you will find is that you've completely let go of your attachment.

The best part about all of this is that when you let go of all that attachment, what you'll find is that you become more attractive naturally. When you aren't pushing for things to happen, you'll find that things tend to happen the way they're supposed to. You may have a goal, but you leave yourself open to something better happening. In the end, you'll rid yourself of any suffering, and you'll be in a healthier mindset to achieve what you want.

Self-limiting beliefs

The biggest thing holding men back from having success with dating and relationships are their self-limiting beliefs. These are the things we tell ourselves to avoid talking to women. You've probably told yourself something along the lines of "she's too pretty for me" or "I don't have anything to offer her" or "She would never go for a fat guy like me."

Some other common ones are "women don't like bald guys," "women only like guys with money," and "women don't want to be approached because men are bothering them." You hear these all the time, but they aren't necessarily true.

Let's take the bald guy one, for instance. How many times have you seen good-looking bald guys like Jason Statham or Bruce Willis with hot women? You can be balding or thinning and still make yourself attractive and appear confident with women by owning the situation and shaving your head. In fact, a shaved head is a very traditionally masculine look that women respond very well to. What they don't like is when guys try to hide it with a combover or a bad toupee.

That is just one example, and I'm sure I could easily come up with a dozen others. The point is that if you see a woman you want to talk to and that little voice in your head tries to talk you out of it, that is more often than not a self-limiting belief.

So how do you handle self-limiting beliefs? The answer is very simple: you challenge them. When you first do this, you will likely be filled with anxiety, which is normal. Just realize that thinking about things causes anxiety but taking action cures it.

If you have a self-limiting belief about approaching women, that they will be bothered if you go up and talk to them, challenge that belief! Set yourself a goal to talk to three women a day for at least three weeks. Keep the goal simple and attainable and go out and take some action to challenge that belief. You'll find that approaching women is often welcomed by most women because a lot of men are too afraid to do it. Sure, some may in fact be bothered, but if you get rejected by one, that isn't a big enough sample size to form a solid enough opinion about your belief.

You should also stop and think critically about the limiting belief you have. Let's say you're a heavyset guy and you think women only date guys who have six-pack abs. Go for a walk around the local mall sometime. Be on the lookout for chubby guys who are with attractive women. I guarantee you'll find them. The same goes with pretty much any other belief that is holding you back.

You might be telling yourself that THOSE chubby guys probably have something you don't have. That, by itself, is a self-limiting belief. Just remember that if one man can do something, another man can do it, too. Why not you?

How to meet women

There are approximately four ways you can meet women, and all of them are solid ways to do it. I don't care what anyone says. There is no single "best" way to meet women. The best way is the one that works for you. There are some pros and cons to all of these, so I thought I would bring those up.

Some of these might sound better to you than others. That's fine. Just know that all of this can be a grind. It's easy for men to get discouraged with the process of meeting women and taking them out on dates, so it's important that you have fun with it, and let go of any attachment to the outcome. The best way to do this is to treat all of it like a science experiment as I've mentioned above.

The first method is often referred to as cold approach, or meeting women in a public space. Essentially, you are out and about in a certain area, you see an attractive woman, and you walk up and talk to her. Many guys think this is the best possible way to meet women, but I've come up with the following pros and cons:

PROS
- You can show her all of your faculties, body language, facial expressions, confidence, etc.
- This will give you a better chance if you're physically not very attractive, but you have an excellent sense of humor.

CONS
- You're essentially working the law of averages with this, which states that the more women you approach, the better your chances will be.
- Not every woman you approach will like you or will be available.

- You're limited to a small geographic area, and the hopes that hot women will be where you are at the time.

The best way to do cold approach, in my opinion, is to get in the habit of talking to everyone you meet wherever you go. Test for interest (more on this later) with everyone you meet, and, generally, just be a social person. This way when you do happen to run into an attractive woman, you will talk to her like you do everyone else. You'll be more natural that way, and you will eliminate any approach anxiety.

The next way to meet women is very much like cold approach, but it's a better option for the modern age: meeting women through social media. Two of the best social media apps for this are Instagram and Facebook because you can send video and voice messages. Here are some of the pros and cons with this method:

PROS
- When using video messages, it's similar to cold approach.
- You have a larger geographical area to work with.
- You can add women to your friends list like it's an Amazon Shopping cart.
- It's a great option if you live in a rural area where meeting people in person is limited.
- Women who accept your friend request are more likely to be interested even before you reach out.

CONS
- You're working the law of averages with this method as well.
- Not every girl you add as a friend will be available.
- Sometimes you will message women who know each other.
- Sometimes you will message married women or women with boyfriends.

- It can be time-consuming adding thirty women a day and going through their profiles to see if they might be single.

There's a lot of potential with this method. I first learned about it from a dating coach friend of mine named Benny who teaches his clients how to do this. He met his wife with this method and built-up a very abundant dating rotation in the Atlanta, Georgia area doing this.

If you've never heard of this method, you essentially look for hot single women in your area. You will check their profiles for relationship status if they have it posted, but if they don't you'll do a quick check of her pictures for other signs that she might be single. Once you determine she's a good candidate, you send a friend request. After at least a week, you will send video messages to the women you added. The message is something simple just saying, "Hey Cindy, this is Paul, your random Facebook friend. I just saw your post about puppies and thought I'd drop by and say hello."

The video message is meant to be a bold move and is essentially very similar to walking up to a cute woman on the street and introducing yourself. This is designed to get a conversation started, and, hopefully, you can segue that into setting up a date.

I mentioned that sometimes the women you do this to will know each other. I have a friend named Luke who would line up all of the girls in his area who had the same name, and he'd make one video to send to all of them to save time. There was one time where he sent a message like that and two girls with the same name happened to be roommates. They sent a joint video back to give him shit about it. He handled it like a shit test, but he didn't get a date with either of those chicks. This sort of thing will happen. I suggest laughing about it and just having fun with it when it happens.

Social circles are another great way to meet women. This one is a little more organic than the first two methods. This is how you can end up dating a friend of a friend. I've met a couple of dating coaches that specifically teach the social circle method and they swear that this is the best way to meet extremely beautiful women. I often think that's just a sales pitch though because you can meet beautiful women using any of these methods. Here are some pros and cons with social circle:

PROS
- It's more organic.
- You already have connections and social proof through your friends.
- It's also great for general networking outside of dating and relationships.

CONS
- It can be a grind to get started.
- The first ten girls you make friends with are off limits for hitting on because you're building your circle and establishing trust.

One cool thing about social circle is if you meet someone new, invite her to the meetup, and if she has a boyfriend already, tell her to invite her boyfriend too. This will expand your social circle, and it gives you easy plausible deniability. Either way, women with boyfriends are usually friends with other single women.

One of my close dating coach friends who specifically teaches this method says that the best thing about it isn't the relationships he makes with women, but the relationships he makes with men. He's been able to travel the world, go on expensive yachts, and do business deals with the men he's met in his social circles.

Another thing that he says about social circles is that the hottest of the hot women aren't out and about to be cold approached, and they're not on dating apps. The only way to meet them is through social circles because they know their value and don't have to find dates and relationships the usual way women do. Maybe that's true, and maybe that's not. I've met quite a few very attractive women via cold approach and via dating apps. I personally think that's just a selling point for his coaching program, but he's a good guy so I give him the benefit of the doubt.

The last method is dating apps. This is my personal favorite because it's the method I have used to meet all of the women I've dated and hooked up with since my divorce. It was the best method for me because I literally live in the middle of nowhere. There are no good places to meet women organically in my area. Most of the women I run into at the supermarket are old and retired!

Besides it being good for rural areas, here are some other pros and cons:

PROS
- Most efficient with time and effort.
- Easy to set up.
- Great option if you live in a rural area where meeting people in person is limited.
- Already established intentions for romantic connections (Nobody is on a dating app to meet friends)

CONS
- If you want a similar experience to women and date passively, you have to pay for premium.
- Catfish.
- Disproportionate demographic of men to women.

There are a lot of men who complain about dating apps, and they say it's impossible to meet high quality women on dating apps. That's not true at all. The truth is that men notoriously suck at using dating apps. Yes, women have more options, and they tend to filter guys out rather than look for matches, but, honestly, that really isn't much different than the dynamic in the real world.

I took my girlfriend out for drinks the other night, and we went to one of the busier bars in the Montrose, Colorado area called **Town Hall Tavern**. The place was hopping with music and patrons and a DJ playing dubstep music from the early 2000's. It was a pretty cool place, and I couldn't help but notice that it was full of about 80% men and 20% women. That's essentially the same ratio you will see on a dating app as well. So what's the difference? In either case, you have to figure out how to set yourself apart from the competition.

The secrets to dating app success

So many guys get hung up on the statistics of dating apps. You hear it all the time online, men lamenting about how 80% of the women are going for the same 20% of men or something to that effect. They cite those statistics as a reason why men should avoid dating apps since the odds are stacked against us.

You also hear people talk about how dating apps are designed to either keep people on the app or keep them coming back. It's a form of marketing churn. The more they keep people unhappy and coming back, the more money they make.

While these things are true, the problem is not the dating app. The problem is that people, particularly men, suck at using dating apps. If men just put in the slightest bit of effort, they would do way better on them. It's not even that hard.

Success on dating apps comes down to four basic factors: the quality of your pictures, the quality of your bio, how you open conversations with women, and how you close for dates. It's pretty simple when you get down to it.

Guys like detailed formulas, so I created a list of the six types of photos you need on a dating app. I based this list off of Rich Cooper's list in his book, **The Unplugged Alpha,** with some slight modifications. If you are stuck, definitely try to incorporate all or some of these ideas into your dating app profile:

1. **A good headshot** - This is just a simple head only shot and is pretty self-explanatory.
2. **A full body shot** - This is important so they can see in what general shape you are in. Women need to see what you're working with. If you are overweight, this lets them know upfront. They will find out eventually in person anyway, so there's no sense in hiding it. In this picture you also want to not be wearing a hat, and you want to smile showing your teeth. If you're bald, again you want them to know that up front. They will find out in person anyway, so there is no need to hide it.
3. **A social proof picture** - This is a picture with you and some of your friends or family members. This tells women you are a people person and other people like you.
4. **An action shot** - This can be a picture of you doing something fun and exciting like mountain biking or backcountry skiing. Women want to join a man who lives an exciting life. This is your chance to show them what your exciting lifestyle looks like. If you don't do anything fun or exciting now, you need to start. It will make you more interesting and attractive.
5. **A mystery shot** - Women love a mystery! This can be a picture of you facing a sunset so only your silhouette can be seen. Or if you are a motorcyclist, you can pose with your bike wearing a helmet. See below for an example of my mystery shot.
6. **Something cute** - This can be a picture of you holding a puppy or a kitten. It gives you that "awe" picture that women like. A lot of guys hold pictures of

dead fish. That isn't cute and women hate it. A live, cuddly animal will help you out much better.

The mystery shot I used on dating apps

If you can afford it, get these pictures taken by a professional photographer who specializes in dating app profile pictures. Make sure they also understand concepts like masculine body language and what women really find attractive. For instance, studies show that women find a more brooding look or even just a slight smirk more attractive than a full smile. This means that you shouldn't be smiling in every picture because that subconsciously tells women that you are a nice guy, and that will turn them off. A lot of photographers don't think about stuff like that.

If you can't afford to hire a professional, then go get a tripod and use the timer feature on your phone's camera app or get a camera that has a timer feature. They also make small gorilla tripods that can wrap around fence posts and tree branches so you can get creative.

The important thing here is that you don't want a lot of selfies in your profile. It either consciously or subconsciously tells women that you don't have any friends to take pictures of you. The idea is that *happening* men have other people taking pictures of them. If that's not the case for you, you can at least create that illusion for your dating app profile.

Of course, all of these rules sort of go out the window if you are in good shape. For instance, I had a lot of selfies in my profile for a while and I did fine because I was in pretty good shape. For instance, here's a selfie I've had on my dating app profile for a long time:

Effective selfie

A few things worked well in this picture, one you can see some definition in my arm, especially my shoulder. Also, I'm outdoors doing something interesting. Notice the waterfall in the back? Remember how women want to join your lifestyle if you do fun and exciting things? It turns out that women find waterfalls fun and exciting. I also think the fact that I was using a selfie stick made it less obvious, and you can see a good portion of my body and what I looked like.

Now that you have an idea of what kinds of pictures you should be taking, let's talk a little bit about style and appearance. I already mentioned that if you are in shape, a lot of the rules go out the window. This is true with style as well. If you are in outstanding shape, you'll probably look good wearing a burlap sack. Most people aren't pinnacles of physical shape, though, and, in all honesty, on dating apps you really only have to be in better shape than the other guys in your area.

For instance, as you can see in the pics above, I am in fairly decent shape, but I am not ripped by any sense of the word. I do not have well defined six-pack abs. That doesn't matter, though, because if you look on the dating apps at the other men in my area, most of them are very overweight, "corn fed" looking country bumpkins. It wasn't that hard to set myself apart by just not being fat.

You don't want to be a slob either. You want to look like you have some fashion sense to set yourself apart from other men. Now, most dating books will talk about the importance of wearing a suit and how wearing a suit makes you look high-value and classy. They also talk about how women love men in suits for those reasons. While that all may be true, you also want to make sure your clothing matches your environment and your personality.

I already mentioned that there are a lot of country bumpkins in my area. That's because I live in a rural area with a lot of farms and ranches. Nobody wears suits out here, even at somewhat classy restaurants. If I were to walk around in a suit, I'd look like a complete dipshit. So that suit advice does not always apply to folks in flyover states.

Some good rules do apply, though. For instance, wearing clothes that fit make a huge difference. Form fitting is best, especially if you are in shape. A lot of men dress for comfort and wear clothes that are too big and baggy. Instead, try to wear clothes that are one size smaller than you're used to.

If you are a big guy and have a spare tire, go back and read the chapter on fitness and diet. Lose that weight. You will do so much better on dating apps if you are fit and in shape. There really is no way around this. In fact, if you can build your shoulders and lats up, and trim your waist, that v-taper is a physical marker of attractiveness that all women look for.

Proper hygiene is paramount. Make sure you are showering with soap and water every day. Women do not like your natural musk, especially if you've spent all day doing physical activity. I went to a live pro-wrestling event with my girlfriend once and there was a wafting smell of body odor from some of the fans there. It was gross. A lot of grown men don't wash themselves, and it is unacceptable. Don't be one of those guys.

I get it, she can't smell you on a dating app, but the goal of a dating app is to eventually meet in person. Get in the habit of having good hygiene and smelling nice. Besides, studies show that the better a man smells, the more confidence he has. Women can actually pick out a man who is wearing cologne and smelling nice in pictures just by how confidently he carries himself. This has been shown in studies.

Facial hair is your friend. It is a marker of testosterone and women find it very attractive. In fact, studies show that women like men with facial hair and the optimal amount is roughly ten days of stubble. So let your beard grow out for ten days, figure out what guide on your electric trimmer keeps it at that length and then try to keep it there.

Your hairstyle is important. You want to find something that is currently in style that also looks good on you. It is worth it to go to a high-end stylist at least once to get a really good cut that fits your face well. Once that is done, have the stylist take a picture of it so you can take it to a more affordable place to keep it looking like that. Most lower-end shops can keep up a good cut as long as they have a picture to work off of.

If your hair is thinning or you're bald, you have a few options. You can get hair transplant surgery, you can take a product like Rogaine that helps you regrow your hair, or you can just own it and cut it short or just shave it off completely.

The problem with hair transplants is that oftentimes they just delay the inevitable. You'll eventually lose that hair ten to twenty years down the road anyway. You also will have to take Rogaine as well to try to keep your newly transplanted hair for as long as possible. The less well-known problem with Rogaine is that it can decrease your testosterone levels, and that will cause other problems like low libido.

My hairline really started to noticeably recede once I got into my 40's, so I weighed all of the options and just decided to own it. I shaved my head. A lot of guys are afraid to do this, but studies show that women actually find fully shaved bald men very sexy. Especially if a man is confident in his appearance with it.

There are two other options I didn't recommend: wearing a toupee or growing your hair out in one area and trying to comb it over the balding area. Neither fool anyone, but both reveal your insecurity about losing your hair, and, frankly, both just look terrible most of the time.

Your oral hygiene is really important, too. You want to make sure you are brushing your teeth at least twice a day. A lot of dentists recommend brushing after every meal which I think is a little unrealistic. So, at the very least brush your teeth in the morning when you wake up and brush your teeth before you go to bed. You want to get in the habit of flossing, too. I personally like those plastic floss picks over regular dental floss. Just figure out what works for you and stick with it.

If your teeth are dingy and yellowing, work on whitening your teeth. Dingy yellow teeth are really common for smokers as well as coffee and tea drinkers. I struggled with yellow teeth for years, until a friend of mine recommended store brand whitening strips. I used them every day for an hour a day, and after a couple of weeks I noticed a considerable difference!

I had never paid much attention to it until I started making online videos, and people in the comments were brutally pointing it out. I'm glad I did something about it, because it gives me more confidence. It also makes sense that I should do that since I often focus on women's teeth and how well they take care of them.

If your teeth are crooked, broken or flat out missing, you need to do something about it. Invest in yourself and get them fixed. If they're crooked, get braces or Invisalign. You can also get veneers, or, if any teeth are missing, I recommend getting implants over dentures. Yes, implants are more expensive, but think of it as an investment in yourself. You might even consider doing it as part of a dental vacation in Mexico where the cost even with traveling is often cheaper than getting it done in the United States.

Now that your pictures are squared away, and you are looking good, let's talk about bios for a bit. The biggest rule of thumb to know when it comes to making an effective online dating bio is that less is more. I've read dating books where the coaches tell the reader to write long paragraphs about stuff, and to paint word pictures. It's largely a waste of time. Women aren't going to read several paragraphs about you. They have too many options to care that much.

You also want to make sure you are keeping your bios upbeat. A lot of guys will write out a laundry list of what they don't want in a woman. For instance, they might write:

> *Smokers need not apply! If you're a single mom, swipe left! No tattoos!*

You get the idea. Doing that isn't helping as much as you think. Sure, the smokers, single moms and women with tattoos are going to swipe left, but so will 99% of the other women who think you're a negative person. Nobody wants to date a negative person.

Here's the bio I used to have in my online dating profiles that got good results. Feel free to use this, but I highly recommend you tweak it to fit your personality and lifestyle:

> **Too many people are trying to rush into relationships. I'm just seeing what's out there until I find the right woman to join me. My ideal match will be into fitness and outdoor adventure like me and will compliment my lifestyle. Is that you?**
>
> **T-shirt and jeans (Or shorts) guy. Don't expect anything else. In fact, my t-shirt collection is borderline absurd... but I own it! 😎**
>
> **I don't have a lot of time for texting but getting to know each other in person is better anyway!**

There's some psychology in the first paragraph that you should be aware of. The first sentence lets women know upfront that I'm keeping things casual to start. The second sentence sets up a challenge for them to qualify themselves to me, and possibly be the one that can lock me down. I'm also setting up the frame that they are joining me in my lifestyle, not the other way around. As a man, you want to be the buyer, not the seller. The third sentence is also a statement that urges them to qualify themselves to me.

The second paragraph sets up the expectation that I'm not a suit and tie guy, and to not expect me to dress up. This is really important if you are a casual dresser like me. Don't pretend to be someone you're not.

The final paragraph sets the expectation that I'm not going to be texting them all day, and not to expect it. A man on his purpose in life doesn't have time for texting, anyway. A lot of losers out there are addicted to texting, and it's a needy, unattractive quality that will turn a woman off. Some women say they want, and like that, but the truth is that if you are spending all day texting, you're a loser. You have nothing else in your life going on, and subconsciously women know that. So, keep texting and phone calls to a minimum, and only use them to setup dates for in person.

The next key to dating app success is how you open conversations with women. There's no "right way" to open with women on a dating app. The right way is the one that gets a response. Some things that have a decent response rate are:

- Be original
- Put some thought into it
- Make an assumption about her
- Playfully tease her about something

Some guys open with something like, "Hey beautiful!" or something copy and pasted like, "You look like trouble." Those openers have zero thought put into them and are unoriginal. 97% of dudes in your area are opening with that, and the women in your area are ignoring them.

Before you get upset about that, put yourself in their shoes for a minute. They have way more options than you do. If you had the number of options they do, you would do the same thing. You would filter out the low effort guys and go with guys who put more thought into what they were saying. Women don't use dating apps like men do. Men are trying to get matches. Women are trying to filter matches out.

I once went to a men's retreat with a dating coach friend of mine, and one of the things I learned at that retreat was about how women use dating apps. He had his wife set up a fake profile, and within a matter of a few hours, she already had over a hundred matches! That's mind blowing to most men because most men may only get 5-10 matches at a time if they're lucky.

We also learned how women look at messages. They are looking at everything in the preview pane in their inbox first. That means you have about seven words to capture her attention. Boring openers are not going to capture her attention.

My go-to opener was to pick one of her pictures and try to guess what she was thinking in the moment. That falls in the category of the third bullet point, *make an assumption about her*. I think this worked well because I had another dating coach friend of mine tell me once that statements get more engagement than questions. That's because if you make a statement that is incorrect, people are very quick to jump in and correct you. If you make a statement that is correct, people often like to agree and explain why you are right. Try it out sometime. It's pretty fascinating, especially on dating apps!

The next thing you need to get good at is bantering via text on dating apps. If your dating app allows you to send voice or video messages, use that feature. I can't stress this enough! Women really dig voice and video messages, and most guys don't use them. They will immediately set you apart from other guys because women can hear your tonality in audio, and if you use video, they can also see your facial expressions and body language. It's also a bolder move, which shows confidence, and women love confident men.

Getting back to banter, though, you really don't want to spend too much time doing this before setting a definite date. A lot of guys think they need to text for several days or weeks to build rapport before setting a date. That's not true at all. The purpose of a dating app is to get off the dating app. Nobody serious about dating wants a pen pal.

Now, banter is an art. You simply want to keep things playful, funny, and casual, and you want to tease her a bit. Whatever you do, don't be boring. If she asks you what you did today, don't answer her seriously about how you went to work and walked your dog. That's boring as hell. Jokingly say that you spent all day tracking down the local crime boss, who happens to dress like a penguin. Obviously, this is a reference to Batman, and is false, but it will make her laugh and will often get her to play along.

Most women live lives of quiet desperation. Their lives are boring and mundane, and they are looking for a guy to liven things up for them. You're goofing around pretending to be Batman on a dating app will give them that excitement even if it's just in the form of text, voice, or video messages.

Another thing you want to realize when texting women is that you want to keep your investment level one notch lower than hers. This is game on a subconscious level, but women can tell when you are over-investing and putting in more effort than she is. This is unattractive to women because they know that guys who are good with women aren't needy and don't have to try too hard.

You can do this by playing what I like to refer to as mirror game. You keep an eye on how long it takes her to respond, and you keep an eye on her text bubble size, and you put in slightly less effort when you respond. For instance, if it takes her five hours to reply to your last message, wait five hours and thirteen minutes to reply to her. If she writes a 4-word sentence, reply back in only two or three words, you get the idea.

What you find is that women who might be responding with low interest at first, start trying harder to get you engaged. You want women to try hard, because that shows investment. If she's not investing in you, she's wasting your time at the end of the day.

All of this playful teasing and joking is going to create H.E.A.T., which I've already mentioned a few times in this chapter. You want to get her Emotional Anticipation and Tension spiked so that she's excited to meet you in person. I usually recommend only bantering back and forth with a woman on a dating app no more than 10-15 messages before finding a segue to set a definite date. This is where closing for a date comes into play.

Before you close for a date, you should have a plan in mind on where you want to take her. Never ask a woman what she likes to do, or where she wants to go. A lot of guys fall into this trap because they think that doing whatever she likes to do is the key to making her happy. It's not though. What makes her happy is a man who is decisive and knows what he wants. This demonstrates masculine energy and allows her to relax into her feminine energy. She doesn't want to make decisions when dating. She just wants to show up looking hot. It's your job as a man to make the plans.

To make things simple for you, I highly recommend always taking first dates to the same place. Have a go-to place that you're familiar with and have a secondary backup location in mind that is close by so you can take her there if you like her and things are going well. She should be the only person on this first date, but you will take many women on this same exact date. Repetition is the mother of skill after all, and you will be more comfortable the more you go on first dates to the same place. On top of that, you will start to learn the names of all the staff which will give you social proof on dates.

Ok, so now that you've been bantering for 10-15 messages, and you have your place in mind, it's time to close for a date. One good way I would do this is the next question a woman would ask me, I would say something like "That question deserves an in-person answer. When are you free to meet up for drinks?"

When she tells me her availability, I would then close by telling her to meet me at my go-to place at seven on the night she is free. This should always be for drinks in the evening because if you want to be a woman's lover, you have to do what lovers do. Drinks in the evening are romantic. Meeting for coffee somewhere is something that friends do. Do you want her to be your buddy, or do you want to fuck? If you want to fuck, trust me, drinks in the evening is where you want to go. Dates, after all, are just fun filled opportunities for sex to happen. I learned that from Corey Wayne.

If you're wondering how to say it, this is how I would tell women to meet me, "You're free Thursday night? Perfect! Meet me at The Feisty Pint at 7pm Thursday."

All she has to do is say yes at this point. You'll find that being direct like this will get you lots of yeses!

Telling her to meet you does a couple of things to create H.E.A.T. that asking her does not. First, it's bold, direct, and assertive. These are all characteristics that most women find attractive in men. Second, it demonstrates your ability to lead the interaction. Women want a man who sets the tone and leads. Third and lastly, this tests her ability to follow your lead, and lets you know if she is compliant. If she puts up resistance to being told what to do, you'll more than likely find that she will be a pain in the ass to deal with, and you don't need that kind of headache.

Once she agrees to the date, the next thing I do as a test of interest is to tell her to give me her phone number. If she gives me her number, this is another sign of interest. If she puts up resistance, she has low interest. I would tell her by saying something like, "I hate using these dating apps. Give me your number."

Once I had her number, I would usually send her a voice or video message over MMS simply saying something like, "Hey this is Paul from the dating app, now you have my number too."

After that, I would get the hell off the phone and the dating app until the night before the date. You really want to save conversations for when you are in person. Texting and phone calls are for logistics. You want to build anticipation for the date, and you can't do that if you are texting her all the time.

One thing to keep in mind about setting up dates is that you don't want to set dates more than two or three days in advance on dating apps. The more time you put between closing for a date and meeting up, the more likely she will flake. Women are notoriously flaky, too, so you can't avoid it completely. All you can do is minimize the odds. Spiking her emotions when you close helps and setting dates only a couple of days in advance helps as well, but it isn't foolproof. You can be the best closer on dating apps, but you should never get excited for a date until she's sitting across from you at your go-to place.

High interest vs little to no interest

This section is one of the most important sections for men to understand when it comes to dating. Often, men project their attraction onto a woman who is not reciprocating that same attraction level. This leads men to over-pursue and even chase. This is needy behavior and is unattractive as hell. Sure, some guys say they like a challenge, but as you get older and wiser you realize that it's a monumental waste of time.

You really do want to choose a woman who chooses you. I believe it was David DeAngelo that first coined that concept. Adam Carolla used to say on his podcast that women who like you will open doors for you, and you just need to be aware of it and walk through those open doors. In short, women who are into you will make things easy for you. Women who aren't interested will be a challenge. Cut low-interest women off quickly and move onto higher-interest women. You'll be much happier that way.

One thing I learned from the late great Alan Roger Currie (ARC) is that there are essentially four types of women you'll run into: reciprocators, rejectors, manipulative time wasters, and wholesome pretenders. In my opinion, the best two out of these four are the reciprocators and the rejectors. The reason being is that neither of them leave you guessing. They make their intentions clear. They're either into you or they're not. ARC told me that he loved the wholesome pretenders the best because he liked the challenge of seducing them. These women pretend not to like you or pretend that they're "not like that" and won't put out on a first date but will show you enough interest to make you seduce them and "convince them otherwise." I can see why a guy would like that challenge. Manipulative time wasters are the absolute worst of this bunch, though.

A manipulative time waster is a woman who knows a guy is interested in her and will lead him on enough to get him engaged, and possibly even spend money on her, without ever giving anything in return except perhaps the fantasy that she "might" someday give in. A lot of suckers get taken in by these women because on the surface they seem like they really are interested. Her words, text messages and body language suggest she's interested. However, her actions are completely contradictory. She says she'll go out with you, but you can never get her to meet up in person. That sort of thing.

It's important to weed these women out quickly. A lot of guys complain about the idea of mixed signals from women, but this is where paying attention to her actions and ignoring her words can be very helpful. A woman's actions never lie. If she is not into you, her actions will tell you everything you need to know. If you only learn one thing from this chapter it should be that you must pay attention to her actions over her words. *Acta, non verba*. Actions over words. Got it?

A couple of examples of mixed signals you might see on the dating circuit would be a girl who says she wants to go out, but whenever you go to set a date she's always busy. Another example might be a girl who says she's not interested in dating but loves to text you out of the blue and see what you're up to. A final example might be a girl who is happy to meet-up and make out, but never wants to go back to your place to fuck. In all of these, her actions are saying that she's not interested.

You can go even further to measure a woman's attraction to you by thinking of it as a scale going from zero where she has absolutely no interest in you to ten where she's madly in love with you. I first learned of this scale from author Doc Love who measured attraction as a percentage going from 0% to 100%, then author Corey Wayne simplified it as a scale of 0-10. Either way, it's the same.

Essentially women with an attraction level below a 5 have no interest in you and you are wasting your time trying to get them to be interested in you. Women you meet on a dating app, or who are receptive when you meet them in person will be roughly at a level 5-6. Based on your interactions with women, you can raise their attraction levels to you. For instance, on a first date you may raise the attraction level to a 6 or a 7. Here you might notice that she's touching you or allowing you to touch her. At a level 7 or 8 she'll really want to get close to you, make out or even engage in sex with you. At a level 9 or a 10 she is basically madly in love with you and wants your attention all the time.

This scale is good to know when you eventually end up in some form of serious relationship because you want to keep her at the 9 or 10 range as much as humanly possible in that situation. Her attraction level won't always be constant at that, and you should always assume a lower level of attraction, but roughly having an idea where she's at will help you calibrate your actions towards her and recognize when attraction is starting to dwindle. More on that in the relationship chapter.

For dating, I'd much rather focus on Dr. Robert Glover's scale. It's much simpler. She's either interested or she's not. It's binary. Don't make it complicated.

Understanding this when dating allows you to be like *The Gambler* in the old country song by Kenny Rogers! The relevant part of the chorus was:

> *You've got to know when to hold 'em*
> *Know when to fold 'em*
> *Know when to walk away*
> *And know when to run*

This can absolutely be applied with women. When they are showing you high interest, you hold 'em. When they are not showing you interest, you fold 'em and walk away. When they exhibit red flags, you run!

When dealing with women, you're essentially testing for interest from them. This applies whether you meet them in person, online, on social media or on a dating app. There are essentially three levels of testing for interest.

At *level one* you are simply starting a conversation. A lot of guys think they need a clever pickup line here. I don't recommend that because pickup lines come across cheesy and canned. Sometimes they make a woman laugh, but most of the time in these cases women are laughing at you rather than at the pickup line. You don't need those lines. Just keep it simple. All you must do is start a conversation.

Level one tests can be direct or indirect. A direct test would be to walk up to a woman, tell her you think she's attractive and that you wanted to say hello. An indirect test would be to walk up to her and casually mention something about your surroundings or ask her a question about something she's wearing. Either one is a good way to start a conversation. That's all you're doing at level one. If she's interested, she'll respond to you and continue conversing with you. If she's not interested, she'll either give you a short reply and move on, or she won't answer you at all. Either way, it will tell you everything you need to know.

If she's not interested, there's no need to get upset. It's not personal. Some people like pepperoni pizza, some like pineapple pizza. You're just not her type of pizza. It's not your problem; it's her problem. Not everybody will like you. Don't worry about it.

Level two testing is a little more organic. If she's engaging with you, conversation will naturally flow into level two. A good way to move this along is to ask her what her name is but not tell her your name. For instance, if her name is Diana, you'd say, "Nice to meet you Diana!" without giving her your name. If she's interested in you, she will ask you for your name. If she doesn't, chances are good she's not interested. A lot of guys offer their name without asking, but this is a missed opportunity to test for interest. Remember, we only want to spend time with women who show levels of high interest!

During level two testing, if she's interested, she'll also be smiling, engaging, and will probably laugh at your dumb jokes. If she's laughing at your dumb jokes, that is a good sign of high interest.

At this level, if a woman is interested, but she's not available because she has a boyfriend or a husband, this is where she'll subtly slip it into conversation. There's no need to ask a woman if she's single. She'll let you know. There are times when a woman might be in a relationship and looking to get out with a much better man, but that's on her, not on you. Your only job is to test for interest and walk through open doors.

You want to keep level two relatively short. You don't want to joke and banter with her more than about 10-15 minutes before finding a segue to level three. This is the same on a dating app. You only want to banter about 10-15 messages maximum before finding a segue to level three.

Level three is when you require something of her. A lot of men stop after level two testing, and it actually leaves women scratching their heads. They wonder why certain guys who are interested don't ask for their number. The act of asking for her number IS a level three test! You are requiring something of her, and in this case, that's giving you her number. A lot of men quit testing for interest before a woman stops showing interest. Don't be that guy, and don't let her down.

With this test I much prefer to TELL a woman to do something rather than ask her for something. There are a few reasons for this:

1. It sets the tone and shows that you are leading.
2. It's bold and assertive.
3. It tests her ability to follow.

A lot of men have a hard time finding a "traditional" or "submissive" woman when dating, but these same men are not properly testing a woman's ability to follow their lead. A woman cannot follow where you don't lead. You'll find that women respond very well to being told what to do. It's in their feminine nature to want to be led by a man. The problem is that most men these days either won't lead or don't know how to lead, which forces a lot of women to be more masculine.

So instead of asking for her number, hand her your phone with the contact app open and tell her to give you her number! We call this in sales, assuming the sale. Also putting the phone in their hand is a powerful move too because they almost can't say no to that.

When I was on dating apps my level three test was to ask when they were free to meet up for drinks. When they told me their availability, I told them to meet me at a specific place at a specific time. I never asked what they wanted to do. I found that I would get more yeses that way. As a secondary test of interest after that, I would tell them to give me their number because I hated texting on dating apps. If they complied, I knew they were most likely interested and they had the ability to follow. Do you see how this works?

Inevitably when doing level three testing you will get the wishy-washy "maybe" response from women, particularly when asking them out for a date or when asking when they are free to meet up for a date. You have to question wishy-washy responses like this using what's often referred to as the Brad Pitt or the Jason Mamoa test. Which is to ask the question, would she say maybe to Brad Pitt or Jason Momoa if they asked her out? The answer to that would be a resounding no. She would figure out her schedule quickly and would crawl through broken glass to make that date happen. Nobody expects a woman to crawl through broken glass for them, but if she's not being upfront with her schedule and giving you a simple yes when she's available, she probably has low interest.

Sometimes women will give you a wishy-washy answer as a shit test or strength test to see how you react. Some guys will get angry and tell her off for not being direct, and they will fail her test. Instead, I recommend doing what's known in sales as a takeaway. It will go something like this:

"No worries, sounds like you have a lot going on. Perhaps another time."

After you give the takeaway, you shut up and wait for a response. You're basically taking your offer off the table because we only want to do business with people who want to do business with us. That's the idea of the takeaway or takeaway sale. If it was a test, and she has high interest, she will figure out her schedule and will give you a clear yes or no instead of the maybe. If she doesn't, you can try again in another week if you want, but often if she's not interested the first time, her interest level won't magically raise the following week. You're better off moving on.

The last thing I want to talk about when it comes to weeding out women with low interest is dealing with flaky women. This is another annoying part of the dating circuit, and there really is no cure for it. Any dating coach that tells you that they have a surefire method for getting women to not be flaky is selling snake oil. There is no cure for it, only coping. There are ways to reduce flakiness, but there is no way to avoid it completely.

When a woman flakes out on you, she'll typically do one of two things:

1. Cancel, but offer an alternative time to meet up
2. Cancel, and not offer an alternative time to meet up

If she does number one, you can tell her no problem and reschedule the date assuming it's within a day or two of the originally scheduled date. If it's a week or two out, just tell her that you'll reach out in a week or two to schedule something. Never set a date more than a few days out, or guess what? SHE WILL FLAKE!

If she does number two, don't even dignify it with a reply. No reply is a reply after all. Sometimes women will cancel last minute as a shit test, and if she has high interest, she will get a strong sense of anxiety when you don't reply at all and will usually correct herself. If it wasn't a shit test, then she really wasn't interested. Either way, it doesn't deserve a reply.

Remember, the goal of all of this is to gauge her interest level, spend time with women who are interested in spending time with you, and cut loose the ones who don't. It's about efficiency, and if you look at it this way, you'll be less affected by the women who show low levels of interest.

On the date

So you met a woman either in real life, on a dating app, or perhaps even on social media. You had the balls to ask her out on a date and she accepted! Well done young man, a lot of men struggle to even get to this point. Now is where your real performance test comes into play. Don't worry though, she wants you to succeed here! She wants you to do well. She is cheering for you, so don't let her down.

The date doesn't start at the venue. It starts in the morning of the day of the date. It starts with you getting up and blasting some music. Music that really gets you pumped up. I'm not talking about relaxing country or reggae music. I'm talking about *gangsta* rap. I'm talking about maybe some heavy metal. Something that you'd listen to in the gym to help you bench 300 lbs.

After your shower, you are going to just look in the mirror for a bit. A full length mirror is best for this, but any mirror will do. You want to look in the mirror and tell yourself that you're a badass motherfucker. While you're doing this, you're also going to do some power poses. By power poses, I mean you're going to stand there and make yourself as big as you can get. Wide stance, wide open arms, big shit eating grin on your face. When I say wide open arms, think of a UFC fighter with his arms open wide begging for his opponent to swing so he can lay his ass out. This will get you mentally psyched up to be the badass, most attractive power player in the dating game.

After your mirror stuff, get dressed and head out of your house. If it's the work week, you'll naturally head out the door for work. If it's the weekend, force yourself to get out of your house and be social all day. Either way, when you go out, you want to talk to everyone you meet. People in elevators, grocery store clerks, baristas, every single person you run into. Whomever it may be, you at least want to say, "Hello, how's your day going?"

Doing all of this will get you in the right mental state to be social. This will get you hyped up to talk to people. This is what is called social momentum and will make you more energetic, confident, and generally more fun to be around on your date. Your date will be able to feel your energy when you talk, and you won't have any nerves because you practiced all day long on a bunch of strangers.

Now let's talk about what to wear on a date. I typically recommend keeping initial dates casual and low investment. That does not mean that you can dress like a slob, or like you normally would on your weekend trip to the supermarket. I am a graphic t-shirt guy myself, but that doesn't mean I would wear graphic t-shirts on a first date. You shouldn't either. You also shouldn't wear shorts, tennis shoes, flip-flops, or anything else like that. You want to put your best foot forward.

Keep it simple here. Wear a nice pair of jeans, a belt that matches your shoes, leather shoes or boots that can be polished, and wear a solid color long sleeve t-shirt, henley shirt, or a button-down shirt. Your button-down shirt can be untucked if it's cut to be worn that way, otherwise tuck it in. You should also wear some nice accessories like a necklace and maybe some bracelets. These are perfect because it gives women something to talk about and even an excuse to touch. Also, for the love of God, wear cologne! A good smelling man drives women wild. I personally recommend Duke Cannon proper cologne. It's inexpensive, it lasts all day, and I have yet to meet a woman who didn't love it. You can get free shipping on orders over $25 by visiting **http://duke.comeonmanpod.com**. We talked about general grooming in the dating apps chapter, so I won't repeat myself here. Go back and review that if you are still struggling with that sort of thing.

I mentioned before that I like to keep dates low investment. For me, that means drinks in the evening. Some people recommend coffee dates for the same reason, but I'm not a fan of them. The reason being is that coffee dates send out a friend vibe. If you want to be her lover, do what lovers do. Take her on a date in the evening for drinks. Coffee dates can work out. In fact, at the time of this writing, I met my current girlfriend for a coffee date because that was her only time to meet up since she was working graveyard shifts as a labor and delivery nurse at the time. If you have game, any venue can work, but when you're just starting out I think the evening rule of thumb is good to follow.

Either way, low investment dates are perfect because you are really just trying to learn two things:

1. Do you like her or not?
2. Is she just into you for your money?

The first one is very important because a lot of men are trying to qualify themselves to the women they are sexually attracted to. That is a losing way to date because it makes you the seller and her the buyer. You'll end up coming across as needy and unattractive as you try to prove yourself to her. Instead, flip the script. Be the selector; be the buyer. Make her qualify herself to you. Sure, she has nice tits, but is she an insufferable bitch who is a chore to hang around with? You'll only figure that out if you make her qualify herself to you.

The second one is important as well because a lot of men lead with their wallets. They try to impress women by taking them on fancy dates, fly them to Miami, or pull up in their Ferraris or whatever. Flashing your wealth to women tends to attract the wrong kind of women, namely gold diggers. If you want to find a woman who likes you for who you are, then she needs to discover on her own if you have any money or not. If you offer a woman a drink or coffee date, and she scoffs at it saying you need to take her to dinner, it tells you everything you need to know. She's into you for your money, not your company. Drop her right there!

Speaking of leading with your wallet, I think it's important to talk about who pays for the date. You asked her out, so you will pay. Don't think you are going to further test if she is into your money or not by asking her to cover the tip or pay for half. Look, equality is bullshit. Women only want equality when it suits them, and in dating it doesn't suit them. Asking her to pay will dry her vagina up like the Sahara Desert. It's also about setting the tone and taking the lead. Besides, it's low investment, remember? If you can't afford to pay for a couple of drinks, you shouldn't be dating. You should be worrying about how to get a better job and make more money.

If she offers to pay, oftentimes it's a shit test. Decline. I once had a gal insist on paying and she put her debit card on the table and slid it towards me indicating she was going to pay.

I slid it back and told her thanks, but I was paying. She slid it forward again; I slid it back. She slid it forward one more time, so I put my finger on the card and playfully slid it off the table onto the floor. I was paying! She got a laugh out of that, and I passed her shit test.

I also recommend paying for the second date as well. If she is still trying to offer to pay on the second date, tell her that you will pay for the second date, but if she's interested in a third date that you'll let her plan and pay for the third date. This is also a good test of her interest, because if she does that, she is REALLY into you.

On a first date, you'll most likely want to meet her at the venue. This is especially true if you met her on a dating app. Women don't usually feel comfortable having strange guys show up at their houses, so just tell her where and when to meet you. I used to like to get to the venue about ten minutes or so ahead of time so I could pick a table and scope out the place. I would text her to tell her which table I was at so she could find me. When she walked in, I would stand up, greet her with a hug, and pull her chair out for her. If she was wearing a jacket, I would offer to help her with it.

A dating coach friend of mine, Benny Lichtenwalner, used to recommend waiting outside a venue and walking in with her because it was all about the experience. You can do this as well, but I don't think it's necessary. Do what comes natural to you though.

Now, you have two options when you are meeting up for drinks or even dinner. You can sit next to her or sit across from her. When I think back on it, I did both, but I think I sat across from them more than next to them. Both are effective for different reasons, so again, do what's right for you here. I'll explain the benefits of each, though.

Sitting next to her is more of an intimate experience because you are going to be closer to her. You're also able to touch her, whisper in her ear, etc. If you are going to sit next to her, try to sit on her left side so that when you whisper in her ear, to her, it's in her left ear. I'll explain that in a minute.

When you can touch her, this is part of the three T's that I learned from Dr. Robert Glover:

- Tease
- Touch
- Tell

The three T's are your more valuable tools in creating H.E.A.T. which, you will remember, means Healthy Emotional Anticipation and Tension. By sitting next to her, you are now in a better opportunity to touch her due to her close proximity. When I say touch her, I don't mean like a pervert or a creep either. I'm talking about innocent touching on her elbow, forearm, maybe even her hand if things are going well. Physical touch is your best friend when it comes to escalation and building attraction.

The other two T's, tease and tell, you should have done a little bit of when you first met her and set up the date. That's the bantering stuff, playful joking etc., and you should have told her to meet you instead of asking her to meet you. You can continue this on the date by telling her to pass the salt, etc. If you get the urge to ask for her to do something, tell her instead. Women respond very well to a man who takes charge like that.

The benefit of sitting across from a woman is, mainly, eye contact. Eye contact is almost as powerful as physical touch, especially if you keep eye contact with her left eye. When I say this, a lot of guys get confused, so think of your right eye looking into her left eye. I learned this from David Deida and didn't think much of it when I first heard it, but it's supposed to be her emotional eye. It's connected to the right part of her brain, and that's also where a woman feels inhibition and excitement. If you stare at her left eye and think sexual thoughts about her, she will be able to feel it and she will be drawn to you. It's like she will be mesmerized by it. It's very strange, and sounds like magical mumbo jumbo, but try it out for yourself and see what happens.

Like I said, the first time I heard it, I didn't think much of it, but I had a man on my podcast in the early days named MJ Durkin who reminded me of it. He said that you shouldn't just do this with women. Do this on job interviews, do this when making sales etc. It's a fantastic way to build rapport with anyone and builds a lot of trust!

Now, I don't know if it's that the left eye is really the emotional eye connected to the right part of the brain, or that it just gives you a good focal point to make eye contact in general, and that any strong eye contact itself builds trust and rapport. Either way, it's a game changer and you should try it.

This is very similar to why I told you to sit on her left side so you can whisper in her left ear. I learned this from the late Alan Roger Currie, the author of the book *Mode One*. He said that if you can get into a woman's left ear zone and whisper in her left ear, you could easily seduce her. The reason he gave was very similar to the left eye trick. Her left ear is connected to the right brain, it's the emotional side of the brain, the inhibition side of the brain. Again, whether that's true or not, I don't know, but try it out for yourself because it works.

So now that you are sitting, however you decide to do it, have her look at the drink menu for a bit and ask her what she wants to drink. When the waiter or waitress shows up to take orders, order for her. Ordering for a woman is a very dominant masculine move and is another way you can set the tone and take the lead.

When you are sitting there, you want to be aware of your body language as well. Women are very perceptive of body language, more than men are. So you need to learn to be aware of it as well. There are lots of body language tutorials on YouTube if you want to learn more about it, but in general you want wide open body language. You want to take up space. Arms wide and relaxed. I used to like to throw an arm over the back of my chair if there weren't any arm rests. You want to lean back as much as possible and sit with your legs wide and open. I'm not a fan of bar stools because you can't lean back easily or sit with your legs wide. Try to find a table with chairs so you can do this.

One thing you want to avoid is sitting with your arms folded. This is a very closed-off look, and women don't like that. Try not to lean in too much. You want her to lean towards you a lot. Sometimes that's not possible, so you can lean in for a bit and then lean back to see if she leans in to follow you. That's a good sign.

If she is showing relaxed and open body language herself, one thing you can try doing as well is subtly match and mirror her facial expressions and body positioning. This is known in Neuro-linguistic programming (NLP) as matching and mirroring. It's a subconscious way of building rapport with someone, and it is often recommended that you do this for job interviews and sales because of how comfortable it makes the other person. It works equally well for dates.

Let's talk about conversation here. A lot of guys are worried that they don't know what to say on a date or how to have a conversation with women. That's the best part. You want her to do about 80% of the talking anyway. Women love to talk, so just let them. Your only job is to keep the ball rolling. By not talking too much about yourself, it allows you to stay more mysterious, and if you actively listen to what she's saying and take a genuine interest in what she says, you come across as an excellent communicator and listener. Women are highly attracted to men who listen. More on that in the relationship chapter.

Another magical thing about letting her do most of the talking is that you won't accidentally stick your foot in your mouth. A lot of guys will talk their way out of contention with a woman. You can't do that if you're not doing a lot of talking in the first place! Iron Rule of Tomassi number eight says, "Always let a woman figure out why she won't fuck you, never do it for her." This is so much easier if you keep your mouth shut.

I mentioned before to take a genuine interest in what she says, but also take a genuine interest in her. She is her favorite subject to talk about, so keep her talking about herself, her interests, her dreams and aspirations. Get her to experience good feelings as she's talking as well, and she'll associate those feelings with you. Ask her thoughtful and open-ended questions, but don't just stack questions. As she's talking, ask her to clarify things, occasionally repeat back what she says, make assumptions and statements about what she's saying. This all keeps the conversation flowing naturally without turning it into an interview. Interviews aren't sexy, but conversations are. At least, they are for women. Women fall in love with their ears after all.

When she asks about you, either give her an absurd and playful answer or keep things short, then turn the conversation back on her. Remember, whoever is asking the questions is in control of the conversation, and you want to maintain a little bit of mystery. You do not want to give too much about yourself away. Nothing will make a woman bored of a man quicker than a guy who tells her everything about himself. She wants to live in a love story, and she wants to discover the love story for herself. She doesn't want any spoilers. If she asks what you do for a living, don't tell her you're an IT Director, tell her you dress up like a bat and fight crime at night! Laugh it off, then turn things back on her. Keep her guessing.

Here's the thing, it's been scientifically proven that women are more attracted to men whose feelings are unclear. I first learned that from Corey Wayne, but don't just take our word for it. Google it yourself. The first article that pops up is a scientific study from *The Association For Psychological Science* about it. Women argue against this all the time, but this is just an example of why you shouldn't listen to what women say and just pay attention to what they respond to. They respond to mystery.

So what if you start talking to this girl, and she's rolling her eyes, checking her phone, being rude or just plain being an insufferable bitch? That's the beauty of drinks-only dates. It can be over after just one drink. Finish your drink, ask for the check, pay the bill, and wish her luck in her dating. No need to be a jerk back, no need to call her out on her bullshit. Don't talk, walk.

If you do like her, it's a great idea to have a backup place in mind down the street. After a drink or two and things are going well, tell her that you want a change of scenery and tell her you know a cool place down the road. Pay the bill and walk with her to the second venue.

Here's the thing, women will sleep with you by the second or third date on average. If you take her to two places, her subconscious looks at the second place like it's a second date. This will speed up this process for you. It's like a two dates in one experience. I like to go to a place with a pool table, darts, or good appetizers, if possible, to continue the conversation and escalation. Walking with her also gives you the opportunity for touching. For example, you can hold her hand as you lead her out of the first venue. You can grab her hand and lead her across the street. You can gently put your hand on her lower back as you move to put yourself on the street side while walking. Walking on the street side is an old gentlemen's custom from back in the day of horses and buggies, but it's still appreciated today.

The two dates in one method is also great if you are looking for first date hookups. I personally never set out for first date hookups. I always just looked at first dates as chemistry tests and would try to escalate on the second or third date. Not everyone has that kind of time though. I have a coaching client at the time of this writing who does lighting for some major rock bands when they are on tour. He travels a lot, so he can't be in one place long enough for second or third dates. He needs to make things happen NOW!

If this is you, or you just don't want your time wasted, then you need to plan things out. Try to pick a venue that is walking distance from your place. If you live out in the boonies like I do, then book a hotel nearby the venue you're meeting at. When you invite her back to your house or hotel room, you need to give her an innocent excuse for going to your house or your hotel room. This gives her plausible deniability. More on that in a minute. My go to was to ask her if she was up for a challenge, usually the answer was an excited YES! I would then challenge her to a game of Jenga at my house! I've heard guys ask if a girl wants to meet his dog or tell her he needs to feed the goldfish. Whatever, just have a reason other than sex that requires you to go to your house or hotel.

Let's talk about plausible deniability a little bit here. Women are more concerned with their sexual reputation than modern sexually liberated feminists would have you believe. Women know that their body count is an issue. They know that their sexual purity is valuable to men. Therefore, they don't want you to think they are sluts, and they don't want their friends judging them for being sluts. Because of this, sex must always be the man's fault, and they need plausible deniability. They need to say either, "I just went to his place to play Jenga." Or they need to say, "I don't know what happened, one thing led to another and the next thing I knew…" You get the idea. Either way, it must be your fault and you need to embrace that responsibility and provide her with plausible deniability.

Like I said, when I was dating, my goal on first dates wasn't to hookup. My goal was to treat it like a science experiment and do a chemistry test. I wanted to see if I liked her or not. If I liked her, I always went for a kiss. You must always at the very least go for a kiss. If she's showing high interest in the middle of the date, looking at your lips, etc then you don't have to wait until the end of the date to go for a kiss, but if those signs aren't there you absolutely must go for it when you walk her to her car. Don't ask her if you may kiss her, don't go for a hug or a kiss on the cheek. Lean in and go for a solid kiss on her lips.

Going for a kiss is the ultimate test of interest. 99.99% of the time it has worked out well for me. There were only two times that women responded negatively, but even then, it wasn't terrible. You'll find that most women are receptive to it. In fact, some women will melt in your arms when you do it because it's such a bold and confident move. The women who aren't that into it will lean their heads back or turn their heads to give you the cheek. If that happens, don't get mad, also don't kiss them on the cheek. Just take the hint. They are telling you everything you need to know. Just tell them thanks for a fun evening and wish them best of luck in their dating.

If things went well, you went for a kiss or even ended up hooking up with her, what you absolutely do not want to do is try to set the next date while on the first one. A lot of guys do this, and it comes across as needy. It shows her that you don't have any options. If she asks you out, that's fine, but you can't do this. Yes, double standard I know, but like I said before, equality is bullshit when dating. Get over it.

After you kiss her by her car to end the date, or after you walk her to her car after first night bedroom shenanigans and kiss her there, keep things simple. Tell her you had a great time and that you'll reach out again soon. You want to keep it vague. You want to keep that mystery alive. You want her wondering when or if you will call or text because this builds H.E.A.T.! A lot of the time, that H.E.A.T. will cause her to reach out to you first either by text or phone call. This is where you want to be because this is her beginning to pursue you.

Catfish dates

I think it's a good time to bring up catfish dates since you will definitely find yourself on a few while out dating. This is especially the case when you are doing any kind of online dating including social media dating.

What is a catfish date? It's essentially when the woman you meet online portrays herself as someone she's not. A vast majority of these women are just trying to make themselves appear more attractive than they really are. Some of them are using pictures of someone completely different in order to scam you. In either case, finding these people online is unavoidable.

Let's get the scammers out of the way very quickly. These are very easy to weed out because they won't meet you in person and won't meet for a video call. If they do at the very least meet for video calls, they won't show their faces. With these types, just unmatch or discontinue communication with them immediately. Remember, actions always speak louder than words. If they won't meet up, or their actions are just completely out of the ordinary, drop them. They are wasting your time.

What about the women who aren't necessarily scammers, but they are just not very gifted in the looks department? That, or they're about 30-100 pounds overweight? In both cases, they think that if they can just get you in person that they will make you fall in love with their personality. A majority of women you find online are going to be like this, and how you view it in your mind is everything!

In Corey Wayne's book, *How To Be A 3% Man*, he says that if he walked into a venue and a woman did not look like her pictures, he would turn around and walk out. He said that a woman like that has no integrity, and he doesn't spend time with people like that.

Other guys I've seen online want to hold these women accountable and tell them off and call them names. They get up in their emotions for having their time wasted and get angry at the situation.

Both scenarios aren't the best use of your time in my opinion. If you drive all the way out to a venue just to turn around and go home. Or you go to a venue, yell at some woman who won't change her behavior at the end of the day, again to just go home, all you're really doing is wasting your time driving to and from a venue to only end up jerking off that night alone anyway.

One thing I learned from Dr. Robert Glover's book, **Dating Essentials for Men**, is that it's good to practice dating. He suggested that guys find 12 different women, they could be old, fat, ugly, it didn't matter because it was just practice. Then go on 12 different dates with those women in a 12-week period. The idea was to go out, have a good time and just practice bantering and attractive body language. We talked about attractive body language in the last section.

I found that since there were so many catfish on dating apps, that I didn't have to go out of my way to find these 12 women for practice. Catfish make excellent practice dates on their own, and they come to you. This is a much better use of your time than getting angry and going home. You're already there, you might as well have a good time and use it for practice. Then, on your next date with an attractive woman, you'll know what to do because you've practiced it. You'll have muscle memory down, and you won't have to think about it.

I already mentioned in the last section that we're keeping dates low investment, anyway. This is the perfect reason for that plan because you don't want to invite some fat land whale to an expensive restaurant for dinner. It takes a lot of money and food to keep these heifers at that size after all. No, we're just buying drinks. This also allows you to end things after only one drink so you're not spending too much money, but you still can get some valuable practice in.

When I would find myself in this position, and a woman who I thought was attractive in her dating app profile showed up looking like steaming trash, I would chuckle to myself and just go into practice mode. I would think about Dr. Glover's mantra that you can't hit a homerun in the majors without taking a few swings in the minors. If you have this mentality, then you'll have a much better time on the dating circuit when you encounter these catfish.

Once you experience enough catfish dates, you'll find that most can be avoided. You'll be able to spot them easier because most follow the same patterns. If all of her pics are cropped to just show her face, that is a very clear indicator that she's fat. Most women who are in shape love to show off their figures. Fat cows like to hide it.

Another thing you find are pics of women with nothing but group photos. If you run into this, I guarantee the chick you're talking to is not the hot one in all of the photos. She's definitely the fat one.

One method that is very popular, especially since SnapChat came out, is putting filters on every picture. The worst are the chicks who do the dog filters like this one:

In this example above, you can clearly tell she's a heavy-set girl. She's not really fooling anyone. Still though, some of these women out here have relatively thin looking faces in their pictures and it's a little harder to tell. This gal is holding her weight in her face though, so it's a dead giveaway.

You can avoid these unwanted interactions by just not matching with her in the first place if her profile suggests something is off. Swipe left and be done with it. The ones who will trip you up are the ones who post pictures of themselves from 10 years ago. These are women who used to be thin, then let themselves go. If you just go by pics, it will definitely lead you to a practice date.

Therefore, the best possible way to avoid a catfish date completely is to do a video call. This is good once you've gotten plenty of practice out of your system and are tired of catfish dates. If you really want to eliminate all catfish, before ANY meetup, invite them to join you for a video call as a vibe check. This will typically let you know what they look like in real life.

Still, when on these video calls, if she keeps the camera on her face or uses a filter on the call, that will tell you everything you need to know right there. Just don't ask her out on a real date in person if she does that.

If she ends up not being a catfish after all, the video call will help you build more rapport with her, and you'll have better chances of closing for sex sooner rather than later. This is similar to the multi-venue tactic I talked about in the last section. In either case, video calls can be a very good idea when dating.

I rarely did the video call thing because, to me, even going on a catfish/practice date was time better spent than sitting home alone. Once I changed my mindset about the whole thing, it turned out to be a fun experience either way.

After the first date

I thought it was important to write a section on what to do after the first date. The reason being is that it took me a while to figure out what worked best for me. When I was studying game, one of my main influences was Corey Wayne's book, *How To Be A 3% Man*. The recommendation in that book did not work at all and was pretty vague.

Basically, that book says that after a date you're supposed to not call or text for about a week before reaching out again and trying to set another definite date. The idea is that she needs time to wonder about and think about you. The problem is that waiting that long, from my experience, tends to give women the impression that you're not interested in them and are ghosting them.

After reading Dr. Robert Glover's **Dating Essentials For Men** a few times, I realized that he had a better method. He essentially said to wait until the next day and text her to let her know you had a good time. Then wait a few days to reach out to set another date.

Working with a good friend and dating coach, Benny Lichtenwalner, I learned that you don't want to wait too long to follow up with a woman who is showing high interest. The longer you wait, the better the chances that her interest will fade. So if you had a good time, and you were receiving signs of high interest (she was touching you, laughing at all your jokes, melted when you kissed her, etc.), then the longest you want to wait is about three days max.

Putting this all together, I found the sweet spot. Don't text her after you get home unless she asks you to let her know you made it home safe. Even then, just let her know you made it home and leave it at that. Wait until around 6:00 pm the next evening, or roughly after most people get off work and simply text to let her know you had a good time the previous night. Don't elaborate or try to start another conversation.

What this does is lets her wonder if you had a good time or not throughout the next day. When she is wondering about you, and waiting for you to call or text, this builds H.E.A.T.. Texting around 6pm will give her that dopamine spike she needs while she's hoping for positive feedback without you waiting so long that you miss the opportunity to reinforce her interest before she loses it. After that, wait two to three days to set the next date.

When you do finally reach out, send a voice or video message to break the silence. I recommend calling her attention back to a funny conversation you two talked about when on the date. Another thing you can do is send her a funny meme first, then follow up a few minutes later with your voice or video message. Both of these will cause a positive emotional spike when she sees your messages.

When she replies, you are essentially going back to square one like when you first chatted with her on the dating app, or when you first got her number. Then you are only going to banter back and forth no more than 10-15 messages before setting the next date.

Some women will be so anxious and unable to contain their excitement that they will reach out to you first. I have found that a lot of women wouldn't get to this spot until at least after the second date, but quite a few couldn't wait that long. This is a great sign. This is her chasing you. When a woman reaches out between dates, she will rarely ask you out directly but will put herself in a position for you to ask her. Just assume she wants to see you again, find the segue after about 10-15 messages, and set the next date. That's what she wants more often than not when she reaches out.

Either way, by making the plans, you are setting the tone and leading. To her, this feels like you are pursuing her even though that's not the case. Much of this game is letting her chase without making her feel like she's chasing. Women are weird that way, but they need that.

For date two, I highly recommend inviting her over to your house to cook her dinner and enjoy a bottle of wine. It's also good to have a fun game or two you can play like Jenga or Uno. My preferred game was Jenga because you could stand next to her and try to distract her by touching her.

If she agrees to dinner at your place, sex that night is pretty much a done deal as long as you don't stick your foot in your mouth and mess things up. Women aren't stupid, and they know that if they go to a man's house, it's likely that the two of you are going to end up having sex. She just needs to know that you're safe, you'll stop if she asks, you won't judge her, and you won't go blabbing to everyone in the neighborhood about it.

Women are very concerned with their reputations, and none of them want to be perceived as sluts. This is why they will tend to feel comfortable about it if you give them some form of plausible deniability like just coming over for dinner and Jenga. This way when you do have sex, and their friends ask, she can lie and say nothing happened, or say something along the lines of "One thing led to another..."

I'll get into sexual escalation in the next section, but for now just make sure you have a logistical plan to make sex a very strong possibility. If for whatever reason you don't close the deal on date number two, don't beat yourself up over it. You'll almost definitely close on date three. Most women will sleep with a man by the second or third date. Just know that if you can't close the deal by date number three, you're wasting your time. She's trying to negotiate desire, but you are looking for women with genuine desire for you, and you can't negotiate genuine desire.

After date number two, you will pretty much follow this same formula until she brings up "the talk." Women who like you will usually push for exclusivity by the 7th or 8th date. Don't ever mention exclusivity yourself. Wait until she brings it up. If you bring up exclusivity or try to put a label on things before she's ready, you will come across as weak and needy. Your only job is to bring the fun, and plan things out so you have the opportunity to have sex. That's it. That's all you do until she wants to have "the talk." I'll address this in detail in the Long-Term Relationship Chapter.

Sexual escalation

There are a couple ways that I'm aware of to get a woman revved up enough to want to have sex. It's important to know these things because if you want to be successful with women at all, you must be able to move things to the next level and make it feel natural and comfortable for her. Guys who don't do this tend to end up in the friend zone.

Let's talk about the friend zone for a minute. A lot of men complain about being in the friend zone, but they are the ones who put themselves there. These men think that women don't want men to be sexual, or they're afraid she will see him as a creep if he tries to push for sex, so they play it safe and treat her like a friend. If you are treating her like a friend, she has no choice but to treat you like a friend back, and that's how you end up in the friend zone. Once you are there, it's difficult to get out unless you know how to sexually escalate.

One of the things I learned from Dr. Robert Glover is that women don't fuck a man they get to know, they get to know a man they want to fuck. Women know men want sex and pretending you don't just makes you look weak. Women actually find men who own their sexuality and don't apologize for it more attractive.

One method that I learned about in my studies is essentially the Mode One approach. This is a method of verbal seduction developed by the late Alan Roger Currie. He talks about this in depth in his third book, ***Oooooh . . . Say It Again: Mastering the Fine Art of Verbal Seduction and Aural Sex.***

If you want to learn that method, I highly recommend that book. In short, Alan would try to get into what he referred to as a woman's left ear zone. I talked about the *left eye trick* and the *left ear zone* earlier in this chapter. The idea is that her left ear is connected to the right side of her brain, and that is the side where a woman's uninhibited thoughts are. Whether that's true or not, who knows? It's worked for Alan and thousands of his students though.

If a woman lets you get close enough to whisper in her left ear, you are in the left ear zone. When you're whispering in her left ear, it's time to be sexual. You want to ask her if whispering in her ear is getting her pussy wet. You want to tell her that her perfume is making your dick hard. You want to tell her that you want to take her to your bedroom and fuck her until she can't remember her name. You get the idea.

Women tend to respond very well to seductive words because it allows their imagination to run wild. Women's imagination and fantasies are your best friend when it comes to seduction. Women aren't typically as visual as men are. They get more turned on when their imaginations are stimulated. It's why cheesy sex novels are really popular with women, but porn videos aren't as much.

Alan Roger Currie firmly believed that you can't possibly seduce a woman without doing it verbally. I disagree, because using his verbal seduction method was not how I would typically seduce a woman. I preferred a type of kino escalation.

What is kino escalation? Kino is short for *kinesthesia* or touching. It's about physically touching a woman in a prescribed manner to both gauge and heighten her sexual interest in you. There is an art to doing this on a date.

When you are just getting to know a woman, you don't want to just reach out and grab her tits, ass, or pussy. This is a sure fire way to get slapped or have a drink thrown in your face. It's also basically sexual assault. Instead, you want to touch her in more innocent places like her elbow or upper arm, her lower back, or her shoulders. One thing women respond very well to is taking her by the hand and leading her across a street or through a crowded restaurant.

When you do this, you are at first testing for interest, and seeing if she's receptive to it. If you go to touch her and she pulls away, you want to pull back, too. She's not ready for it yet. Don't apologize! Just pull back and continue the conversation a bit and try again later. This is called *two steps forward, one step back*.

You want to be doing two steps forward, one step back even if she is receptive to your touching. You also want to be doing this as soon as you have the opportunity while on your date and do it throughout the entire night to build that H.E.A.T. until she just can't take it anymore.

You'll start off with more innocent touching like I mentioned before, but eventually you should move to more intimate, yet still relatively innocent, touching like a kiss on the lips or the back of her neck. Continue to do this sort of thing until you're ready to take her back to your place to provide a venue for the seduction.

The best way to get her back to your place is to ask her at a high point in the date if she wants to come back to your place. You want to give her plausible deniability, as mentioned previously, so she feels comfortable coming back to your place while having a possible excuse to tell her friends and, more importantly, to justify it to herself. I liked to challenge women to a game of Jenga at my place. Jenga is perfect because you can stand next to her when playing, and playfully touch her as a form of distraction to mess up her ability to play.

At some point when playing, you want to go in for a passionate kiss. She is more than likely really primed for this by now if you've been touching her and pulling back little by little all night. Now is the time to start touching her more sexually. Slip your hand under her blouse and caress one of her boobs. Play with her nipple until it gets hard. If she's letting you do this, try taking off her shirt and start kissing her on her neck.

If all of this is going well, she's into it and not trying to shut you down, grab her hand and lead her into the bedroom. If she follows, it's pretty much a done deal at this point. Be sure to have condoms nearby so you're not fumbling for them and killing the momentum like an idiot!

During all of this, a key point is that close proximity is paramount. I distinctly remember failing to seduce a woman because I was playing things too safe and sitting too far away from her. She came over to my house and sat at one end of the couch. Instead of sitting next to her so I could easily touch her, I sat at the other side of the couch. I typically like sitting at one end or the other with an arm rest. I basically chose comfort over sex that night, and she decided to leave before I could make a move.

The next date we had, I didn't make that mistake. I made sure to sit next to her and did the two steps forward with kino escalation and ended up making out with her on the couch and carrying her to my bedroom to seal the deal.

By sitting close to her, this gives her an opportunity to touch you as well. Women who are into you are looking for an excuse to touch you, so help them out a bit. In addition to sitting close, it's not a bad idea to wear accessories like bracelets and necklaces that women can reach out and touch as well.

I once had a date with a woman where I was talking a lot with my hands, and she used that as an excuse to grab my hands and hold them. She told me I had to stop trying to land airplanes. It was her way of playfully saying I talk with my hands too much, but really just gave her an excuse to touch me.

Later that date we got up to go order drinks from the bar, and she stood really close in front of me and was nestling her butt against my crotch. She knew exactly what she was doing. Women don't just do that. I had no idea what I was doing at that point in my post-divorce dating experience though, and thought she was just being nice. I thought, "She seems friendly. I think I'll go for a kiss at the end of the night."

Luckily for me she was extremely forward and ended up basically attacking me in the parking lot of an Applebee's. She walked up and just started making out with me. Most women won't do that, though. You have to be the one to recognize her signals and make the move yourself. I was just happy to get lucky that night.

When you are dating and trying to sexually escalate, you will inevitably run into last-minute resistance with women. A vast majority of the time, this is a shit test. Besides their reputations, a big existential fear women have is being put in a dangerous situation with a man who doesn't know when to stop. No woman wants to be assaulted. So a very common thing women will do is to stop you in the middle of making out and say something along the lines of how she's not ready.

When a woman does this, stop what you're doing and pull back. Don't get mad. Remain indifferent about it, smile, and just continue the conversation. Don't apologize for it either. Just say "no worries," talk to her about something else, and try again later. This is part of two steps forward, one step back. This will let her know that you'll stop when asked, and that will make her feel safe enough to move forward.

If you try again later, is she still putting up resistance? If so, you might try one more time before packing things in and taking her home. You never want to force yourself on a woman. It's an excellent way to land in jail. You also never want to show that you're upset and bothered by it. Getting mad will ruin any possibility of trying again the next time you see her. Always be playful, calm, and indifferent about it.

I've mentioned previously that most women will sleep with you by the second or third date. Largely this is an arbitrary rule they set for themselves, so you don't think she's a slut by doing it on the first date, and so she doesn't feel slutty. If she's putting up this kind of resistance on the first or second date, don't sweat it. You'll more than likely succeed on the third date. If she still doesn't want to have sex by the third date, you really need to move on from this woman. She just doesn't have genuine desire for you.

Here's a very important thing to know about women's natures. They will make rules for guys they are not that sexually interested in, but will break rules for guys they are sexually interested in. That's why she makes the good guy wait until they're married, but she'll fuck the bad boy biker in a Waffle House parking lot. If she's still making rules for you by the end of date three, she's just not that sexually into you. Remember, you want to walk through open doors. You don't want to bang on closed ones.

Spinning plates is the most efficient way to date

The concept of spinning plates, or *plate theory*, is scary to a lot of guys. I think it's partially because we've been socially programmed to think this is wrong, that it's dishonest or somehow disrespectful. This social conditioning only benefits women as it allows them to exercise and weigh their options, but men are often shamed for doing the same thing. Men call it spinning plates. Women just call it dating.

What does it mean to spin plates? The term comes from carnival acts that would spin plates on the top of long dowels or sticks. They would put a plate on the stick, spin it, then put another plate on a stick and spin it. Eventually the guy spinning the plates would have a number of sticks with plates spinning. Some plates would fall off, but for the most part he would usually have at least a couple of plates spinning at the top of several sticks.

The concept can be applied to dating when you are essentially juggling multiple women at the same time. Think of them as plates spinning on top of sticks. Some fall off. Hell, sometimes they all fall off at once, but you keep finding new plates and putting them up on the sticks and keep them spinning. As long as they're spinning, they basically stay on the sticks.

Pretty much every woman you have your heart set on has herself a roster. Women are natural plate spinners. She may not be sleeping with all of them, but she's certainly keeping several on standby just in case something falls through with the man she's currently with. This is very common when a woman is just dating non-exclusively, but even tends to happen when a woman becomes exclusive or even gets married.

According to a Daily Mail article from 2014 by Deni Kirkova, half of all women have a fall-back partner on standby:

> *Half of all women have a fall-back partner on call should their current relationship turn sour, it emerged today.*
>
> *A substantial percentage have kept another man in mind in case they end up single.*
>
> *And married women are more likely to have a Plan B in the background than those who are just in a relationship.*
>
> *It also emerged the back-up is likely to be an old friend who has always had feelings for the woman in question.*

> But other candidates are an ex-boyfriend or ex-husband, a colleague - or someone who they have met at the gym.

You can find the full article at ***https://is.gd/FallBackPartner***

Am I saying that you should have backup options once you get into an exclusive relationship just because women typically do? Not necessarily. My point is that it benefits you to assume women are doing this to you when dating, and it doesn't benefit you to be "the good guy" and not do it in fear of scaring a woman off.

The best part about spinning plates is that it won't typically scare women off. An interesting characteristic of women is that they tend to be more attracted to a man with options. They don't necessarily like it waved in their face, but if you can imply you have other options by keeping your time and attention scarce, she'll assume you have other options. This works in your favor when building up a rotation.

Some men prefer to be upfront and tell women that they are seeing other women. You can certainly do that, but women often communicate covertly and through subtext. Sometimes it's better to do the same when dealing with them in regards to dating other women. The reason being is that you can use her imagination to your advantage. Sometimes it's best to let her hamster wheel turn and get that competition anxiety built up without you having to really say anything. By being upfront with her, she doesn't get that option and might bail as soon as you mention it.

There's a really great book in the men's space that is made up of a compilation of old forum posts by a guy going by the handle of "Pook." ***The Book Of Pook*** is the name of the book. Here's one great quote from it that is relevant to the topic at hand:

"Women would rather share a high value Man than be saddled by a faithful loser." ~Pook

A man with options, a man that other women want to be with, is considered high value to a lot of women. On top of that, women are naturally competitive. They want to win the heart of the man who has other options. She wants to be the one chosen out of his many options. This competition anxiety tends to cause women to invest more in you. The more she's invested, the better she'll treat you.

A lot of men focus their time and attention on one girl at a time. They go all in on her, and when it doesn't work out or they get rejected, they get depressed because they have to start the process all over again. Rollo Tomassi calls this dating with sniper mentality.

Think about it for a minute. A sniper waits in the distance, his target lined up in his sights. He's calculating windage and distance. He's figuring out elevation and velocity. He's putting in all of this effort for one clean shot.

Rollo also refers to spinning plates as dating with a shotgun approach. If you've ever used a shotgun, you know you don't have to be that accurate with it. You just have to point in the general direction of the target, and you'll probably hit it. That's because a shotgun shoots out multiple pellets at once in a scatter formation. Spinning plates works in a similar fashion.

Many guys think that managing multiple women is difficult because they have a hard enough time dealing with one woman. That's because that one woman is their only access to sex. If they mess up, they'll lose out on the sex. So they are constantly calculating what they need to do to not mess things up in order to keep that access to the sex, very much like a sniper calculates the perfect shot.

A guy who is spinning plates doesn't give a rat's ass if he does something to cause access to sex from one girl to stop because he is usually talking with two or three other girls. His options aren't limited, so he doesn't have to invest all of his energy and time into one critical, perfect outcome, the achievement of which defines whether he is successful or not. Instead, he takes a different path to success that is more about abundance than perfection, very much like using a shotgun.

One of the biggest problems with dating with a sniper mentality is that it causes what's known as oneitis. Oneitis is an unhealthy fixation on one particular woman, and that fixation tends to come across in your words and actions as needy. Neediness and desperation are major turn-offs for women. Spinning plates eliminates the feeling of neediness because you aren't needy if you have plenty of options. Funny how that works, right?

Another problem with oneitis is that it causes men to have an unhealthy attachment to a particular outcome. Sometimes that outcome is sex, sometimes it's some form of long-term commitment. It doesn't really matter what the attachment is. The problem is attachment itself.

I'm not a Buddhist, but Buddha taught that the root of suffering is attachment. Spinning plates allows us to let go of any attachment because we have multiple options. If you are dating multiple women, you have multiple sources for sex or potential relationships. It allows you to be the buyer and no longer the seller. Without that attachment to outcome, you can actually remove the suffering other guys tend to undergo when dating women.

Women will come and go when you are spinning plates, but that's okay because once you get good at it, you realize there's always another woman. Corey Wayne compares it to buses. A new one comes along every 15 minutes. You will realize this in your own mind and life when you spin plates, resulting in an abundant mindset when it comes to women, and that mindset is the real key to success in dating and relationships.

I read a really great book on sales once by Grant Cardone called **Sell or Be Sold**. In that book, he says that salesmen don't get upset when they lose a sale to a particular customer. What they're really upset about is that they didn't have enough potential leads in their pipeline. Dating is like sales if you think about it, and spinning plates and making sure you always have new women is like keeping a pipeline full. If you lose one sale, it doesn't matter because you still have the pipeline to work with.

This is all well and good, but most guys have a hard enough time getting one woman let alone a rotation of women. How are you supposed to build a rotation of women so that you can start spinning plates? The answer is to fake it until you make it!

Before you get multiple women, you must first get one. In getting the first one, you will need to act like someone who already has options. This is where fake it until you make it comes in, which I will explain ways of doing that shortly. Until you secure one woman, you must still go prospecting using one or all four of the ways of meeting women mentioned previously. Once you get one, you will just keep going with the process of meeting new prospects, selling up dates and seducing them until you've built up a rotation of women you can manage.

This part is where a lot of guys fail. They start talking to one girl and stop prospecting. You can't do that until you've built up a rotation. If you start talking to one, cool. Keep swiping on the apps, keep cold approaching, keep going to parties, keep adding girls on Facebook and Instagram. Do not stop until you've built up your rotation.

Another big part about fake it until you make it, is the illusion of already dating multiple women. Don't worry, this is just an illusion until you actually start dating multiple women.

Remember when I said that women often communicate covertly, and that you shouldn't be upfront with a woman that you're seeing other women? Knowing this is the best way to get started. Use her imagination to your advantage! If you imply by your actions and demeanor that you are seeing multiple women, this makes you more attractive due to pre-selection. If a woman asks you if you're seeing other women, just be vague and say something like, "I always have room for one more" with a wink. If you flat out tell a woman that you aren't seeing other women, you might as well tell her you don't fuck. It does not help you out.

Another thing that I found helpful was to avoid setting dates with women you've just met on Friday or Saturday nights, and also stop replying to texts and phone calls after 6 or 7 pm on those nights as well. Do this even if you have nothing going on. The reason being is that those are prime date nights, and attractive guys with options always have something fun going on at those dates and times. Usually that fun includes spending time with beautiful women. Women know this, so when you aren't setting dates with them on those nights, their feminine intuition tells them that you have other options. You want to reserve those nights for women who you are sleeping with. Think of it like they have to earn time with you on a prime date night.

Guys with options don't spend their time calling and texting all the time either. So you really want to be using texting and phone calls for logistics only to set up actual dates. Texting and phone calls are not for building rapport. You can only really build rapport in person anyway.

If she texts you, don't be rude, reply back, but use it as an opportunity to set the next definite date after about 10-15 messages, and then end the conversation. This sub-communicates that you are a busy and happening guy with things going On. This will create more H.E.A.T. with her because she's forced to wonder why you are not blowing up her phone.

A lot of this really comes down to letting her hamster wheel do all your legwork for you. The more she is wondering about you, thinking about you, and questioning what other girls you might be talking to, the more H.E.A.T. is being created because her competition anxiety is going out of control.

If you do this to multiple women at once, it really won't be too long before you have a decent rotation of women who are all vying for your attention.

Women will bring up exclusivity by the 7th or 8th date

Many people believe that love and relationships are spontaneous and happen over time--a sort of luck of the draw situation. The funny thing is that when you study, practice and watch this play out around you as well as in other people's relationships who are on the same path. You find that there is nothing spontaneous or random about it. Most of it can very much be predicted based on observing human behavior and studying psychology.

What you will find is that when you are spinning plates and limiting your interaction with a particular woman to one date a week, that by the 7th or 8th date she will probably start pushing for exclusivity. She might even tell you that she's developed feelings for you or has fallen in love with you. You'll know she's at this point if she wants your attention all the time, is texting you all the time, and when you see her, she can't keep her hands off you or jumps in your arms.

Whatever happens, play it cool. You don't want to push for a relationship or be the one to say "I love you" first. One of the

of Red Pill, a guy who went by the name of
_,, broke it down in his first of sixteen *Laws of Poon*:

Never say 'I Love You' first.

Women want to feel like they have to overcome obstacles to win a man's heart. They crave the challenge of capturing the interest of a man who has other women competing for his attention, and eventually prevailing over his grudging reluctance to award his committed exclusivity. The man who gives his emotional world away too easily robs women of the satisfaction of earning his love. Though you may be in love with her, don't say it before she has said it. Show compassionate restraint for her need to struggle toward yin fulfillment. Inspire her to take the leap for you, and she'll return the favor a thousandfold.

Your only job until she brings up exclusivity is very simple. I like to refer to it as FFF or triple F's which stands for Facilitate Fun & Fuck. Your job literally couldn't be any more simple. When she reaches out, assume she wants to go out with you and set a definite date. Make the plans, facilitate fun for you both, then plan the logistics so you can fuck afterwards.

If you are the one trying to push for a relationship, you are working against her hypergamous nature. You are acting needy and projecting low value. A high value man with lots of options doesn't want to be locked down. So if you are readily giving up your autonomy by making a fast commitment, subconsciously you are telling her that you're not as high value as she thought you might be. You're sub-communicating that you have no options, so you're trying to secure her as your only option.

Briffault's Law maintains that "the female, not the male, determines all the conditions of the animal family. Where the female can derive no benefit from association with the male, no such association takes place." From the human perspective, the idea of a relationship must come from her perceived benefit of being in an exclusive relationship with you. You can't push the issue. She has to come to this conclusion on her own.

What if you don't want to be in an exclusive relationship with her? This might be the case if you are spinning multiple plates, and you are spending time and hooking up with women who don't check all your must-have boxes in your **Contender's List** that I will talk about in the next chapter.

If this is the case, remember that men are the gatekeepers to relationships. She can ask for exclusivity, but you don't have to grant her exclusivity if you don't want it or are not ready. If you don't want to be exclusive to her for whatever reason, simply tell her that you are not ready to be tied down, and you like the way things are. Leave it at that, and don't offer any explanations. The ball is now in her court whether or not she wants to keep things going as they are, or if she wants to end things and move on.

Don't be afraid of losing her, because if you are afraid of losing her, this is a tell-tale sign that you've developed oneitis and is also a tell-tale sign that you haven't spun enough plates. Once you've spun enough plates, you really won't care what happens here, especially if you didn't want exclusivity with her anyway.

Some guys at this point might feel bad about this, but you really shouldn't. Remember, she's more than likely doing the same to you. Weighing options is just part of the game. You are not obligated to be exclusive to her just as she's not obligated to have sex with you. All of this is a choice.

If you do want to be exclusive to her, then this is a good spot to be in. You don't want to assume anything, though. Remember, women communicate covertly. She'll be subtle oping you take a hint. She'll say things like, "so .ᵤ ᵤⁿis relationship going?" or something similar. You want to get her to spit it out and be clear about what she is asking. You want her to be more overt in order to avoid falling for her shit test to see how needy you really are.

Ask her what she means by her question. She might say things like, "I know you're talking to other women. I don't want you dating other women." Get her to clarify that statement. Keep asking her what she means until she says that she wants you to be exclusive. Have fun with this though and tease her. Ask her if she expects you to toss out your little black book and ask her if she'd be cool if you kept a backup copy just in case. Obviously keep this playful and fun though, which should come naturally because if you want to be exclusive, this will be a very happy moment for you. Congratulations!

Conclusion

This has been a very long chapter, so let's wrap up with a brief conclusion of all of this. Everything comes down the triple F's of *Facilitate Fun & Fuck*! The whole goal of this is to improve your results by being more attractive, and less unattractive. What I mean by that is be more attractive physically, and not unattractive with your demeanor, attitude and actions.

You also improve your results by being more efficient when you date multiple women at once, learn how to use hypergamy to your advantage, and change your mindset of dating from being the seller to being more of the buyer.

When you have gotten good at all of this, you won't have to think about it anymore. It will be a part of who you are. You will have become *The Game* itself, and you'll have a much easier time in life. Especially when it comes to dealing with women.

LONG-TERM RELATIONSHIPS

Contenders List

Before you get into a long-term relationship, you need to make sure that the girl you get into that relationship is a contender. I'm a professional wrestling fan, and before someone can challenge for a title, like the WWE World Heavyweight Championship, they must earn their place as the number one contender. The same thing goes for any woman who wants to be exclusive with you. She must earn her spot.

A lot of men make the mistake of getting into a long-term relationship with the first girl that's nice to him or touches his dick. This is a scarcity mindset that would be eliminated if you properly spun plates as laid out in the previous chapter. If you find yourself wanting to lock down every girl you go on a date with, it means you haven't spun plates long enough. Go back to the drawing board.

The process to find a woman who could be a contender, and testing to see if she qualifies is relatively simple. Besides dating and spinning plates, you are going to make a list of the qualities you want in woman who you will consider for a long-term relationship, and you will make a list of qualities you don't want in a long-term relationship. You will do this on the same sheet of paper, with the qualities you want on the left side, and the qualities you don't want on the right side. You can also do this digitally on a spreadsheet and save it on your computer. Do whatever works best for you.

Above the column of qualities you want, start it off with:

I am grateful for a woman with the following qualities...

If you recall from The Law of Attraction chapter, using *I am grateful for* is putting you in the important attitude of gratitude. You will be using this list to attract a woman that fits the qualities you want. We are also going to be writing a list of qualities we don't want, but we're not going to focus on those. We're going to focus on all the qualities we want, because we get what we focus on in life. By focusing on the list of qualities you want, you will be engaging your reticular activating system, and you'll start to notice more potential women that fit your list's criteria.

I didn't talk about this in The Law of Attraction chapter, but one of the reasons hyper-focusing on the things you want works, is that it engages what's known as your reticular activating system. The reticular activating system is like a traffic cop in our brains. It's a bunch of nerve cells in the brainstem that decide what information is important for us to pay attention to. This system helps us stay awake and alert by turning on specific parts of the brain when we need to be focused. The reticular activating system also helps control our sleep and wake cycles. Think of it as a filter that helps our brains sort through all the things happening around us, so we can concentrate on what really matters.

Imagine your brain is like a detective trying to solve a mystery. The reticular activating system is like the detective's assistant, helping to filter out unimportant details and highlight the crucial clues. When you train your brain to focus on specific things, it's like giving instructions to the assistant detective. By consistently paying attention to certain details or goals, your reticular activating system starts recognizing their importance. It's like saying, "Hey, brain, these things matter to me!"

As a result, when those specific details or goals pop up in your surroundings, the reticular activating system signals your brain to pay extra attention. It's a bit like having a spotlight on what you've trained your brain to notice. This heightened awareness can make you more likely to observe and recognize things that might have previously slipped by unnoticed. So, training your brain to focus on particular things can help you become more aware of them in your everyday experiences.

When you are sitting down to write out the list of qualities you want, I want you to think of at least ten. You can do more than that, but I think ten is enough to start with. Be sure to write down personality traits you want too, not just physical traits. You'll want to add physical traits as well, just remember that when beauty fades, naggy, bitchy and all around insufferable are forever.

After you write down ten qualities you want, you will do the same thing with your don't want list. In each column I want you to highlight your top 5 must haves in your want column, and top 5 deal breakers in your do not want column. This is important, because if a woman does not meet the criteria in your top five must haves, she cannot be a contender for an LTR. You can still have fun with her, but she is not a contender. Plain and simple. Likewise, if a woman matches any of your 5 deal breakers, you need to end things with her right there. The list is law, gentlemen.

A lot of men mess this up, that is if they do it at all. What they end up doing is writing out their list, then any girl they meet, they try to fit her into their list of wants. Often, they are trying to fit a square peg in a round hole. It's not going to work, and that is not what the list is for. The list is to test to see if a woman ALREADY fits the characteristics of your list. If she does, great! If she doesn't, then she doesn't. Don't try to force things.

By being very strict on the list, you will avoid ending up in relationships that should never have started in the first place. You will avoid all sorts of frustration and heartache by just being a little more selective.

Your list should look something like this:

WANT	DON'T WANT
I am grateful for having a woman with the following qualities...	
Long brunette hair	Short/colored hair
Caring and nurturing	Selfish
Big perky breasts	Flat chested
A dark sense of humor	Easily offended
Highly sexual with me	No sex unless married/exclusive
Good teeth	Bad hygiene
Trim and fit	Frumpy
Conservative politically	Liberal
Life in order	Life's a mess
Good with money and finances	Crushing debt

The examples above are things you can start with, but you need to personalize your list for your unique tastes, and desires.

Love letter to your future LTR

Another thing you can do to attract a better-quality woman, if you want to use The Law of Attraction, is to write out a love letter to your future girlfriend. Using all the qualities in your want list to describe her, and to help you visualize what she will look like. You will write this letter in the present tense, as if you and her have been together for a while already.

Doing this will help make it more real in your subconscious mind, and if your subconscious believes something is true, it will actively work to make it true. You'll start noticing more women that look like the woman you imagined in your letter. It's not magic, it's your reticular activating system pointing them out to you. These women were always there, you just didn't notice them before.

When you write out this letter, you are really going to pour your heart and emotions into it. You are going to want to paint word pictures and be very descriptive so that you can clearly see what she looks like in your mind's eye. You are going to be very descriptive about making love to her, how she looks, and why you are in love with her. The clearer and more descriptive you are, the better.

Writing out this love letter is optional, but it will help to hyper-focus on more of the types of women you want and avoid the women you don't.

There is no finish line

It is important for you to know that there is no finish line. Some guys go into dating with a goal of getting a steady girlfriend. For them, just having a girlfriend is the finish line. Once they do, they think that they don't have to try anymore. Then there are some guys whose ultimate goal is to get married and have a wife and children. They work hard during the girlfriend stage, and when they finally put a ring on it, they think that they've crossed the finish line and can quit pulling forth effort.

In either of these situations, the truth is you're just beginning. The work never stops, because when you stop working at being attractive and not being unattractive, she eventually loses attraction for you and leaves. Statistically speaking, women initiate breakups more than men and they most certainly file for a majority of divorces.

Let me again remind you of Briffault's Law:

> *The female, not the male, determines all the conditions of the animal family. Where the female*

*can derive no benefit from association with the male,
no such association takes place.*

Because of this law, she is the ultimate determiner of
whether you remain in a relationship. Like it or not, men
have a burden of performance. In regard to the relationship,
that means you can never stop working on yourself and
making yourself the most attractive man you can be.

Don't confuse this with putting her on a pedestal and trying
to do things to placate her, make her happy, and avoid
conflicts to keep on her good side. No, the work you put in
must be always on yourself. As Jonathan Hogwood says,
you must always work on your muscles, money, game, and
frame. She needs to see you as her best possible option to
use her hypergamy to your advantage.

Game on hard mode

If you've done everything I told you to do in the dating and
spinning plates chapter, your ongoing self-improvement
won't be as hard as you think because you've done a good
job at filtering your options down to a good long-term
relationship contender. Still though, being in an exclusive
relationship does offer more challenges.

When you are spinning plates and dealing with multiple
women, it's much easier to let one go when she isn't acting
right. If one girl begins acting out of pocket, you simply
remove your time and attention from her and give it to the
women who are treating you right. A lot of the time, if women
see that you have multiple options, they stay on their best
behavior because they are naturally competitive with other
women in the sexual marketplace, and they want to be the
woman you choose above all of the others.

Once you choose them, though, and agree to be exclusive,
they often feel like they've locked you down and they no

longer must compete. Often, society ensures this mentality as well by telling men they must continuously qualify to her in order to make her happy so that she will stay. This allows women to get an inflated sense of worth in the relationship, and often causes them not to try anymore.

On top of that, if you also stop working on your attractiveness, start falling into her frame, and start slowly agreeing to her terms and conditions, she starts to lose respect for you and even starts to resent you.

Probably the toughest thing to deal with out of all of this is that she will see you at your worst. She's going to see you when you're sick. She's going to know when you have diarrhea. She's going to know when you're having a crappy day at work. At these times, how you handle it will determine her attraction and respect level for you. I'll tell you right now, most men don't handle these things very well at all, then complain when women leave.

Having an exclusive relationship is game on hard mode. That is, until you become such a natural at it that game becomes a part of who you are. Once you reach this level, your relationships will feel effortless because the work you must put in is just a part of what you do anyway.

It's best to do this from the beginning

A lot of guys find their way to books like this after a failed relationship or two when they are trying to figure out what they've been doing wrong. When that guy was me I realized that the reason most of us end up here is because we got lazy and complacent. We thought we had reached the finish line and didn't have to try anymore.

Some guys will realize this when their sex lives are in the trash and are trying to get their girls to fuck them again; some guys when they get dumped and are trying to get an ex back; and some guys after they get dumped and want to learn how to do a better job attracting new women.

In all of these cases, the work is the same. You have to work on your physical attractiveness and your behavioral attractiveness. Like maintaining a good physique, it's much easier to keep your game on point than it is to relax on your laurels and try to rekindle a fire that has already gone out. If you find yourself here because the flame has already gone out and you're blowing on the coals to get it going again. You will find that doing the work to make yourself more attractive and not be unattractive will either: bring her back around or put you in a better position for the next relationship. There is no downside to working on yourself.

She's not your mom, best friend, or therapist

A big mistake men make once they get into some form of long-term relationship with a woman is they try to make her their de-facto mother, their best friend, or their therapist. Your girlfriend or wife is none of those things to you and can never be those things for you. She may be your kid's mom, but she's not your mom. She's not your friend, she's more than that. You don't fuck your friends, generally speaking. She's most certainly not your confidant or therapist. Even if she's a licensed therapist, she doesn't want to hear your bullshit.

Whenever I say this to guys, they get upset. They just don't understand that these are not her roles, and she doesn't want to fill these roles for you. She's your lover, and she needs to be treated as such.

A lot of men eventually stop hanging out with friends and pursuing their hobbies and passions because they want to spend all their time with their girlfriend, and they think she wants this as well. It kind of makes sense why guys think this because when a woman is in love she often wants his attention all the time. The catch-22 here is that if you give her your attention all the time, she loses respect for you over time. A woman cannot love a man she doesn't respect. Save her from herself by not falling into the trap of giving her all of your time and attention. Maintain friendships and your interests outside of the relationship. This will make you more attractive because she must still compete for your time and attention, giving her a mission of her own.

One of the biggest mistakes guys often make is dumping all of their baggage and problems on their woman. It makes sense, too, because they stopped hanging out with their friends and have essentially isolated themselves in the relationship. Who else do they have to talk to about their problems? Just her, so they want their women to hold them, console them or commiserate with them. They want her to be their peace!

This dynamic was perpetuated on an episode of the television show *Sons of Anarchy* when character Clay Morrow was having a very stressful time managing the biker gang, so he laid his head on his wife Gemma's lap. He wanted her to treat him like his momma when he had a little boo-boo. This isn't sexy and it isn't sexually attractive. Don't do this! In the show, they presented this as normal, but Hollywood tends to perpetuate this idea that women want to nurture their men, but in reality women subconsciously see this as weak behavior that dries up their vaginas.

Many a man these days treats his girl like she's his best friend. He'll watch girly shows with her, get manicures and pedicures with her, even have pillow fights with her! Okay, maybe not that far, but men often look at their girl like she's their best friend. The thing is that you have a different dynamic with your friends, especially guy friends, than you do with your girl. If you start treating her like one of the guys, you start losing the attractive qualities that made her sexually attracted to you in the first place. She starts seeing you as just one of her really good friends, then sure enough the sex starts to slow down because she doesn't fuck dudes in the friend zone. Key word friend. You essentially end up in the friend zone in your own relationship!

Now, I'm not saying that you can't have fun with her, but mentally you must always keep in perspective of the role she needs to play in your life. She's your lover first and foremost! That means you can have fun with her, but you must always be fucking her, too. That's the game in a nutshell.

If you're making any of the mistakes I mentioned here, be warned: this is why women slowly start mentally fading out of love. It's because you've stopped being the sexually charged man who she fell in love with, and you started optimizing the beta comfort traits that make her feel good but don't make her pussy wet.

She loses respect for you because in her subconscious you are now behaving weak and submissive. A woman's evolutionary psychology and biology won't let her stay with a weak man, so she will start looking around at her orbiters, pick one, and ultimately leave. Many women start doing this up to two years before actually ending the relationship, too, so a lot of guys never see it coming.

To prevent all of this, don't treat her like your mom, best friend, or therapist. Treat her like your lover, set the tone, take the lead, and save talking about problems and struggles for your friends.

If you don't have any boys to talk to about your struggles, consider joining my Beer Club. It's an online virtual men's group where guys can talk about guy stuff and have an outlet for their struggles. We have meetups every month. Learn more at **http://beer.comeonmanpod.com**.

Keeping attraction going long term

There is a natural polarity and order to any relationship. A vast majority of men and women have been taught a reverse idea of how this works over the last sixty years or so due to the rise of feminism. Oddly enough, gay and lesbian couples understand this better than anyone. In order for there to be a healthy relationship, one person needs masculine traits and the other, feminine. Feminism has taught women to embrace masculine energy and behaviors in order to compete in the career world, and men have been taught to defer to their women's leadership in the relationship world, which in effect has made men more feminine. It all goes against our evolutionary nature.

Have you ever noticed how hard it is for women to lead and make decisions? Just ask a woman what she wants to eat, or what outfit she wants to wear. It's almost impossible for them to do it. When a man comes in and sets the tone, leads, and makes decisions, it really sets him apart from other men these days. Women see this and naturally relax into their feminine nature. They may all be boss bitches in the office, but the last thing they want to do when they come home is be in charge. The sooner men realize and take advantage of this, the healthier and longer lasting their relationships will be.

Think of your relationship as if it were a United States warship. The man in charge of everything is the Captain, or Commanding Officer (CO). The next in command is the Executive Officer (XO). Both of these positions are leadership positions, but at the end of the day, the CO is in charge of the ship. If the Officer Of The Deck runs the ship aground, it's the CO that gets relieved of duty, not the XO. The XO may make suggestions from time to time, and the CO might take those suggestions under advisement, but at the end of the day the crew is going to do what the CO orders, and the CO is ultimately responsible for the crew's performance.

You must have this mentality in your relationships as well if you want your girl to respect you. If you defer to her, she will start losing trust and respect for you and a woman can't love a man she doesn't respect.

The best way to describe this is with the age old "where to have dinner" debate. A lot of guys don't care where they eat, and they want their girls to be happy, so they ask her where she wants to eat. Women hate making decisions, so she throws it back in his lap. This can go on and on. Instead, don't ask her where she wants to eat. Just pick a place. If you don't particularly care where you eat, it should be easy. Just think of two restaurants and flip a coin. Then tell her to grab her cute shoes and tell her where you are taking her. Ever since I started doing this, all I've ever heard is "Okay, sounds good."

A lot of guys are afraid that they'll pick the wrong place, and she'll get resentful and use it against him. Being afraid of your girl's emotions is another thing that makes you look weak in her eyes, and that weakness is what truly causes resentment. She resents settling with a man who crumbles under her emotional storm instead of being a man that stands firm.

Now, some women will not like the place you pick. If this happens, simply ask her if she has a better suggestion. If she has a legitimate suggestion, and since you probably don't care, anyway, there's no reason to not go with what she suggests. If she says that she doesn't have a better suggestion, and she just doesn't like the place you picked, stand firm and tell her that you're going to the place you picked and she's welcome to join you. She can take it or leave it. I guarantee she'll either go grab her shoes like you said, or she'll try harder to come up with a better suggestion.

There is a difference between leading and being controlling. In the previous example, if you were controlling and she said she didn't like your choice, you'd simply tell her to shut up and that you didn't ask. I'm not saying that at all. Like a CO would take his XO's suggestions under advisement, you can take your girl's suggestions under advisement too. However, if you don't like her suggestions, then shrug them off for what they are… Suggestions.

Another part of this dynamic of being the leader and setting the tone is to do chivalrous things for your woman. Open doors for her. Walk on the street side of a sidewalk, that sort of thing. I do not let my girlfriend open doors for herself. If we go somewhere I have her wait until I walk around the car and open the door for her. This sets you apart from most men as well because a lot of guys don't do this anymore.

Some guys think doing these things is putting your girl on a pedestal. It's not. These acts are all about setting the tone and leading the relationship. You are performing these acts as part of your rules, not hers. Doing these things also tells her that you are in charge and have things under control. This helps her relax into her feminine role more and builds trust and respect.

Some of this goes back to doing the three T's, which I mentioned before. *Tease, touch, and tell* are the three T's. Teasing her, and treating her like a bratty little sister, helps you maintain a position above her in her mind. Touching her periodically helps you with seduction which is important for both short term and long-term attraction. And telling her what to do keeps her in her feminine because feminine women are naturally submissive. I talk about this in the dating and spinning plates chapter, but a lot of what we're doing with maintaining attraction long term is to always do what we did in the beginning.

Above all, you must constantly maintain your frame. Rollo Tomassi's first Iron Rule:

Frame is everything. Always be aware of the subconscious balance of whose frame in which you are operating. Always control the Frame, but resist giving the impression that you are.

What is frame you may ask? The best explanation of it I've ever heard is from a guy going by **strategos_autokrator** in the Married Red Pill subreddit. He described frame as being a tetrahedron, or a tripod, where the base is made up of physical, emotional and intellectual pillars. These three pillars come to a point, and at the point is your vision. If a man loses frame easily, it's because he doesn't know what he truly wants (Vision) or one of the base pillars is weak. Maybe he's physically or emotionally weak. Maybe he lacks knowledge of game and attraction.

Rian Stone says it well in his book, **Praxeology: Volume I | Frame**:

> *Frame isn't something you do. Frame isn't a thing you have. Frame is who you are. Frame is formed by your physical, intellectual, and emotional selves which provides a stable foundation for you to structure your vision, your goals.*

To over-simplify it, I like to think of frame as how you see the world. Anything outside of your frame is funny or amusing. Once you have good frame control, which does include elements of everything above, you'll have better control over your emotions, how you think, and how you respond to things around you. Having good frame control is paramount if you want to maintain attraction in the long term.

I mentioned before that your woman is not your mom or your therapist. This is important to understand if you want to maintain attraction long term. Your woman expects you to be her rock. It doesn't work the other way around. Women may think they care about your problems, they may even want to care about your problems, but their evolutionary DNA won't let them.

What does that mean? It means that your girl will come to you with her problems on occasion, and when she does, she wants you to actively listen. She doesn't, however, want you to solve her problems. Women work through their problems by talking things out and expressing their feelings. They really just want you to be a sounding board. This is challenging for men because we're hard wired to solve problems. Once you realize that she doesn't want you to though, and it's not your responsibility, it can be very freeing.

If you ever find yourself in a place where you aren't sure what to do, just ask her if she wants your advice or just wants you to listen. More often than not, she just wants you to listen. In that case just pay attention, repeat back some of what she says, and ask clarifying questions.

One thing I learned from Dr. Robert Glover is that often women go off on unnecessary tangents when telling stories about the day. They'll tell you every minute detail about every interaction she had, and all the interactions the other people in her story had. Men don't tell stories like that very often. When men tell a story, it's usually linear and they get to the point quicker. Women are all over the place. When a woman is telling you a story like that, it's perfectly acceptable to playfully ask her to give you the "guys version" of the story to keep her on topic and to get to the point. Doing so is showing her that you are setting the tone and leading the interaction as well. She'll appreciate you for it.

The key thing to remember here is that when she's having an emotional breakdown, she doesn't want you to join in. If she's lashing out, she doesn't want you to lash back. You have to be like The White Cliffs of Dover, and her emotions are like the raging seas crashing against them. The rocks are immovable, as you must be in those moments. She doesn't want you climbing on her emotional rollercoaster.

She needs to know that one of you has their feet on the ground. That is your job as the man and the masculine leader in the relationship.

As you progress in your relationships with women, you'll notice that they will test you. I talked about this in the dating and spinning plates chapter. We call these tests strength tests or "shit tests." Always keep in mind that women test men, not to be shitty, but to make sure men have their shit together. The more you pass her tests, the less she will test. A good friend of mine once said that it's only a shit test if you fail it.

The difference between shit tests when you're dating versus when you're in a long-term relationship differ in magnitude. For instance, if you're just dating, a woman might playfully make a jab about your height. When you're in a long-term relationship, your girlfriend or even wife might get some crazy idea to remodel the kitchen at the cost of $20,000. How you handle each of these determines the respect level she has for you.

In this instance, simply being stern and telling her no is enough to handle this kind of test. She may argue why it would be a benefit, but if you stay firm and remain indifferent to her emotional reaction to you telling her no, then you will pass this test. You can even apply some amused mastery here, too. If she gets upset about it, just tell her she looks cute when she's mad, and pull her in for a passionate kiss.

Another way she might test you is when she gets a random negative emotion out of nowhere and lashes out at you about something random--about how you never buy her flowers, let's say. If you scramble to buy her flowers, you might think you're calming the situation, but, in reality, you are caving to her demands. The answer here is to remain unaffected by her emotions. You can acknowledge them and tell her you understand how not getting flowers makes her feel. Or you can playfully agree and amplify with a quip about how you wanted to buy her flowers, but the flower shop only had dandelions. But whatever you do, don't rush out and buy her flowers.

When women do this sort of thing, it really isn't about the kitchen needing remodeling or her needing flowers. It's her testing to see if you will climb on her emotional roller coaster or not. If you climb on, you fail. If you keep your feet on the ground, you pass.

The funny thing about this is that when a woman gets all emotional, and a man stands firm in the face of her emotional storm, this builds H.E.A.T.. A lot of guys go out of their way to squash any kind of discontentment from their girl, but, in doing so, they kill any form of healthy emotional tension in the relationship, and that will kill attraction long term.

Rollo Tomassi's Game Maxim 27 says:

> In the absence of indignation, women will actively manufacture it for themselves.

Dr. Robert Glover also says that one of his ex-wives once told him, "If you can't stand up to me, how am I supposed to trust you to stand up for me?"

The fact of the matter is that women love drama. Why do you think they watch chick flicks and romantic comedies? Why do you think women love gossip? If women don't have any drama in their lives, they create it themselves. Which brings me to Rollo's 29th Maxim:

> Indignation is a woman's drug of choice, you must become her drug dealer.

The long and short of all of this is that handling her tests effectively when she does these things is a great way of demonstrating your authority in the relationship and continues to set the tone. Doing this will make her feel safe and secure in the relationship. If you're the one that supplies her indignation in a controlled way, she will become addicted to you.

Another key aspect of keeping attraction going long-term is that your girl needs to feel a bit of competition anxiety. She needs to know that you're still an attractive man who other women want. The absence of this is a big problem in a vast majority of long-term relationships and even marriages. Once you put that ring on her finger, she feels like she doesn't have to try anymore. Why should she? You're not going anywhere.

When you're just dating and spinning plates, she knows that you can leave at any moment for some other girl. This tends to cause her to step up her game a little bit to ensure that you pick her as your best option. This is essentially using her jealousy and mate-guarding response to your advantage.

In order for that attraction to be maintained for the long term, you have to keep that going. Now there are right and wrong ways to do it. You can do toxic, active dread where you are actually cheating or at least giving the illusion of cheating. Or you can do more passive dread where you just carry yourself as an attractive man, you stay social, you don't dissuade women from flirting with you, and your girl notices it because women tend to be perceptive when it comes to those behaviors and situations.

I here's some examples of toxic dread ideas that might work, but I don't necessarily recommend:
- Post photos of you and other girls on your social media.
- Take a random photo of a masculine drink, like a glass of whiskey or a beer next to a clearly feminine drink like a margarita or a daiquiri and post that on social media when on a business trip.

- Go to the perfume counter at Macy's and spray on women's perfume. When your girl asks you about it, blow her off, or just say you were sampling perfumes.
- When at a party with her friends, make suggestive comments to her friends and let it get back to your girl.
- Make her a very romantic dinner, with candle light, wine and ensure it's very memorable, then go no contact for two weeks.
- Have an affair, let her find out and confront you about it. Make sure it's not at your house. When she confronts you, let her vent and don't say a word. When she's got it all out of her system, tell her she's never looked more beautiful and you'll never stop loving her, then leave and go no contact for two weeks.

Do you see how these might be problematic? I got these ideas from Christopher Canwell and Roissy. I have the impression it might work on certain girls with abandonment issues or something, but on a healthy girl with self-respect, you are more than likely going to sabotage your relationship for no reason.

I much prefer and recommend the idea of passive dread game. This really takes very little effort on your part, because you should be doing most of this already. You see, the same stuff you did to attract her in the first place makes you a more attractive man to other women as well.

Instead of playing dumb, active and toxic dread games, you simply do the following:
- Go to the gym and stay fit.
- Maintain a healthy diet.
- Stay well-groomed, and always use cologne.
- Always keep an eye on your body language and try to use dominant masculine body language everywhere you go.

- Talk to everyone you meet, and always look into their left eye when making eye contact.
- Always stay funny and flirty, especially around other women.
- Always be a gentleman around your woman and do things like opening car doors for her.

What will happen is other women will see this sort of thing in action and will start checking you out. You may not notice it, but your girlfriend or wife certainly will.

A study was conducted by the School of Psychology at the University of Lincoln in the UK that proved how women often check each other out, sometimes more than men. They do this as part of mate selection, where they are judging their own attractiveness in relation to other women around. A part of that includes other women's reactions to their man.

If other women are giving you the eye, believe me, she will notice, and that will cause her to be more attracted to you and up her game in order to keep you.

The last thing you want to do in order to maintain attraction long-term is what I like to refer to as ABS, or *Always Be Seducing*. A lot of men run into the problem where they want their girlfriends or wives to initiate sex more. They want to feel like she wants them just as much as they want her. The problem with that is that you're acting like a woman when you do that.

I get it, we all want to feel wanted. You have to understand that women aren't wired for that. Men really aren't either, but most men nowadays are raised to be defective women because of a feminist social order that has conditioned us since birth. You have to break out of that way of thinking if you want to maintain attraction long term.

Instead of waiting around for her to initiate sex, because you'll wait around forever in some cases, you need to initiate more. It really is a simple concept. If you want more sex, initiate sex more.

Women are passive by nature and expect men to take the lead with this. A fun side effect is that the more you initiate, and the more orgasms you give her, the more she will initiate on her own. You have to take the lead with that, like with anything else.

You also want to do kino escalation with her every chance you can get. When you walk behind her, slap her on the ass. I like to think that not slapping her on her ass is disrespectful. When she's cooking, or folding laundry, walk up behind her, grab her around the stomach and kiss her on the back of her neck. Stuff like that.
When you're in normal conversation with her, or swapping the occasional text message, always sprinkle in sexual innuendo. Doing so keeps sex on her mind, almost as much as it is on your mind. This also gets her mental fantasies to work for you when you're not having sex with her.

Always keep doing the three T's: touch, tease, and tell. *Touching* is the kino escalation. *Teasing* is just being playful and can include the sexual innuendo we just talked about. *Telling* her what to do shows dominance and leadership which also is attractive to her. All of this builds and maintains H.E.A.T.

Finally, you want to keep dating your girlfriend or wife. A lot of guys get in a long term relationship and get lazy and complacent. They stop doing fun things with their girl. They stop taking her out for fun activities, or even worse they schedule a specific date night and do the same thing for it every week, which becomes predictable and boring.

You have to remember, either you take your girl on dates, or some other guy will. So keep doing what you did in the beginning. Plan fun date nights, change things up, and keep her guessing when you will do it. Occasionally, plan mystery dates where you just tell her what to wear, but don't tell her where you're going to take her. This builds anticipation and excitement, all of which builds more H.E.A.T..

A lot of guys look at this sort of thing as work, but if you change your mindset and perception of it to more of an outlook of having fun, then all of this sort of thing will become effortless for you.

Communication is not the key to healthy relationships

You often hear in popular culture, and from modern psychology, that communication is the key to success in a relationship. This isn't necessarily true. The reason is that men and women communicate differently. Men like to argue to figure out the truth. Women want to argue to win. Men typically communicate rationally. Women typically communicate emotionally. Men are just looking at what's being said in the moment. Women are looking at other subtextual communication queues like tone and body language. Relying on communication as the primary key to ensure success in relationships is, at best, ineffective.

Another factor is that women just want a man "who gets it." It's one of the reasons women shit test men, to make sure that his actions aren't just a facade and that he's truly the masculine man he's portraying himself to be. If she has to tell a man how to act or what to do, that means that he doesn't inherently "get it" and he's probably not the strong masculine man she thought he was. This eventually kills her attraction.

On top of this, communication, at least in terms of how relationship counselors recommend it be practiced, tends to be a negotiation of desire, but you cannot negotiate genuine desire. If you have to tell your girl to fuck you more, and she retorts with, "You need to do the dishes more and perhaps I'll think about it," then there's no genuine desire there anymore. It's why the concept of Love Languages is bullshit. It ends up being a negotiation for desire, and a covert contract where you or she are trying to do something in the hopes that the other person will give you what you want.

The problem here is that if you think about it, in the early stages of a relationship you didn't have to negotiate anything to get her to want to fuck. She wanted to fuck all the time, because she had genuine desire and attraction for you. More communication won't get you back to that, attractive actions and seduction will.

A lot of guys who find themselves in this stage of the relationship have usually gotten very complacent. They've stopped doing the attractive things they did in the beginning, and they've been consistently failing shit tests. This has caused her to lose not only attraction but also respect. A woman cannot love a man if she doesn't respect him.

Demanding respect doesn't work either. You can't demand that she respect you. What are you going to do? Give her an ultimatum? Respect me or else! An ultimatum is a declaration of powerlessness. It means you've run out of all options.

So what usually happens when a woman stops respecting her man and has lost all attraction is that she starts really acting shitty. She starts nagging all the time. She talks shit about her man in front of others. She starts flirting with other men.

A lot of men who find themselves in this spot resort to arguing and giving ultimatums thinking they're the same thing as boundary setting, but they aren't. She will perceive any form of demands or negotiating as whining which just confirms her lack of respect because she sees you as weak. Verbally confronting her is basically an admission that you can't control the situation. In this case, it becomes validation seeking. You are asking her to validate that she cares enough about your feelings by complying with your request. It gives her all the power.

If you've let things get this far, then the only course of action for you to take is to not talk about it. Demonstrate your strength by walking away. Women will respond more favorably to a demonstrable act of strength than to any kind of verbal exchange you force her into. Again, women don't communicate the same verbally, but physical action is universal. This will show her that you won't tolerate her shitty behavior.

If she continues afterwards, never be afraid to leave her permanently. Michael Yon once said that the strongest negotiating power is being willing to walk away and mean it. That's something you have to demonstrate, not threaten.

In a long-term relationship, you always want to reward her good behavior and punish her bad behavior much like you would a small child or a puppy. If you want to train her to be a good girlfriend or even a wife for you, this is how you do it. A lot of guys think that if their girl is withholding sex, then they'll punish her by withholding sex from her. All that does is gives her a mental pass to go fuck the neighbor. She will not go without sex, but you might. Instead, if she does initiate sex, you want to reward her for doing so by fucking the ever-living shit out of her and giving her leg-shaking orgasms. Let her know she's being a good girl.

If she's acting out of pocket, punish her not with words or violence. Doing so is just a display of your loss of frame. Instead, punish her by removing your time and attention. Attention is the coin of the realm in girl world, so removing your attention and presence is one of the worst punishments you can inflict.

Finally, in relation to all of this, there may be times when your girl needs a little space. I'm not saying when she comes up and says she needs a break from the relationship, but just a little space for her to collect her thoughts. If she says she wants a break from the relationship, it means she wants to test the waters with a new suitor, and you need to just break-up with her. If she's just pulling back a little, you need to pull back too.

A lot of guys will notice their girl is pulling back a little and realize that something is off in the relationship. What they end up doing is they chase after her and try to talk things out. The problem is identical to when you chase anything in the wild: it tends to run faster.

Instead, think of your relationship like you and her are holding a rope. In order to keep H.E.A.T. going, you need that rope to remain tight. That's the healthy tension part in the H.E.A.T. acronym. If she's pulling away, and you chase after her, the rope will go slack. This represents the lack of healthy tension in your relationship. Her pulling back is her attempt to apply tension in the relationship.

Chances are, if she's at this point, you've already let the rope go slack in the relationship. So if she's pulling back, you either need to do nothing and let her pull it tighter, or you need to pull back too and apply tension yourself. Pulling back at the same time she does will apply that tension faster.

Never forget that familiarity kills attraction, but space creates attraction. Don't be afraid to allow a little space to come into your relationship in order to keep that attraction alive. You've probably heard that absence makes the heart grow fonder. It's absolutely true.

You don't need to get the government involved in your relationship

A lot of men are raised to think that the inevitable end-state for a relationship is state-sanctioned marriage. They especially believe this if they want to have children and raise a family. This is simply not true. There is no need to get the government involved in your relationships, and for men there is zero benefit to do so. Some people might argue that there are tax incentives, but I guarantee those aren't really worth it. Talk with an attorney, but there are plenty of other ways you can get almost exactly the same benefits of being married without actually being married if you have legal instruments like power of attorneys, wills, and trusts in place. You can even add non-family members as beneficiaries of your life insurance if you want.

Once you have kids with a woman, having or not having a marriage license doesn't really change anything. As long as your name is on the birth certificate, your child is still your child. The only difference, depending on the state, is that you won't have to pay alimony if you break up. You may still be on the hook for child support, however. A marriage license, prenuptial agreement, or some form of trust cannot prevent you from having to deal with child support in the event of a breakup.

Having been married once in my life, I had to learn the hard way. Most men unfortunately have to learn the hard way when it comes to this. Hopefully, if you're a young man reading this, you can learn from my mistake, but marriage only benefits women.

If you're a young woman reading this book for some reason, please do get married! If things don't work out you will be awarded cash and prizes! Depending on the state, you might even be awarded cash and prizes for the rest of your life!

Now the laws aren't typically written to give preference to women, but they more often than not end up that way because of women's hypergamous nature. Women rarely marry men who are below them socially and economically. Yes, there are women who make more than their men and end up paying those cash and prizes to their ex-husbands, but they are the exception, not the rule. Women overwhelmingly end up getting paid child support and alimony after the divorce far more than men do.

On top of that, in community property states, women who didn't contribute a damn thing financially to a household can end up being awarded half the value of a house. This happened in my divorce where I owned a home in California and was the only one making mortgage payments on it for the 3 years we lived in it. When we sold the house, we ended up making $20,000 in profit. When she filed for divorce, she walked away with half despite not contributing anything.

There are a lot more men out there who have gone through much worse divorces than mine, but the financial pain I felt after the divorce was enough to teach me to never do it again. It's like a child who touches a hot stove. Humans often have to experience the pain of consequences, so we know never to do it again.

Here are some things to keep in mind if you do want to have a family someday. I highly recommend it. It's sort of our biological duty to keep the species moving forward after all. Besides that, your children provide you all sorts of joy and fulfillment that money simply can't buy. You just need to be smart about it.

Seeing as how children end up being better off when raised in a household with both the mother and the father present, if having children is the goal, I highly recommend planning on doing it in a state that doesn't recognize common law marriage, is not a community property state, and has a custody default of 50/50 should you and your girl decide to breakup. At the time of this writing, that only leaves you with Florida and Kentucky that meet the criteria of all three. Please do your own research on this and definitely consult an attorney.

Also, please note that I made a distinction between three common types of legislation when it comes to shared parenting. Those three are a presumption of joint custody, a presumption of 50/50 custody and a consideration of 50/50 custody. The best possible option, in my opinion, is a presumption of 50/50. That means it's automatically presumed, whereas a consideration is subjective based on the judge. Likewise, joint custody by itself doesn't automatically mean 50/50 parenting time, It could be 60/40 or 70/30 parenting time.

What does common law marriage mean? It essentially means that if you live together in the same house for a certain period of time and act as husband and wife, the state will treat you like husband and wife in family court. This means your ex-wife can go for things like alimony if she wants to be a vindictive bitch, which oddly enough happens frequently during a breakup.

What does community property mean? It basically means that all property and assets must be divided equally between both parties in the event of a divorce. In my state of Colorado, for instance, we're a fair and equitable state which means that if I can show I paid 100% for a house during the time of the marriage, I'm more than likely going to keep the house. In a community property state, that doesn't matter. She gets half the value no matter what.

What does a custody default of 50/50 mean? It means that the state has a default presumption that children's time will be divided equally between parents by default unless circumstances can be shown where that doesn't make sense. There's states where 50/50 is considered, but that doesn't necessarily mean it's done by default. Kentucky was the first state to add that law to their books, and Florida just added it at the time of this writing.

One option you might consider if you're religious is to have a ceremonial wedding with custom vows. I've known guys who have done this, and they didn't get the state involved. This is an option too, just know that verbal vows are meaningless in court. Women mean till death do us part in the moment, but not necessarily twenty years down the road.

Having the church preside over marriage was in wide practice up until about 1920, according to the book *Dilligaf: Truth About Marriage in The USA* by my good friend that goes by Retired Goat. It was around 1920 where states began to issue marriage licenses to keep Black people from marrying white people. Fascinating, isn't it?

If your girl insists on getting the government involved, point out that little nugget and see what she says. In either case, just know that once you get Uncle Sam in your bedroom, he gets to decide how you break up.

MARRIAGE AND CHILDREN

For some of you, traditional marriage complete with the marriage license is going to be the goal. You've been raised this way forever and it's ingrained in your values. I get it. You have to do what you think is right for you.

Just like I said in the last chapter, always contact an attorney before moving forward with this. Settling down with a woman is the biggest decision you can make as a man. Nothing in this world can make or break a man like getting married. Either you followed the advice in the dating and spinning plates chapter and thoroughly vetted her to make sure she really is a good choice for long-term commitment, or you tried to fit the first girl who touched your dick into your idealistic fantasy, and you are making the biggest mistake of your life. If you do the latter, she can absolutely ruin you.

This is why it's so important to talk to an attorney about protecting yourself, your assets, and your access to your children should the marriage not work out. There are a couple of ways that I'm aware of that can help, but almost nothing is bullet proof.

The first option you can exercise is to draw up a prenuptial agreemont. I hear men all the time talk about how judges throw these out. I've talked to family attorneys who say that the reason these get thrown out, or parts thrown out, at least, is due to how they were executed. If you present your girl a prenuptial agreement written by your attorney on the day of the wedding, she can argue coercion. However, if you present it to her months before the wedding and have her retain her own council to review it, then she will have a hard time arguing that.

Prenuptial agreements also get thrown out because guys go cheap and write something on a napkin or go to an online site like Legal Zoom to get them done. If you want a better chance of it working, spend a thousand dollars or so to have an attorney draft one up. This is definitely one of those things where you get what you pay for.

What I like about prenuptial agreements, regardless of their effectiveness, is that they make ideal shit tests for women. If she is willing to sign a prenuptial agreement, it shows that she has skin in the game. If she refuses to sign one, it tells you everything you need to know about her.

Another option is to put your assets in an irrevocable trust before getting married. A trust is a separate legal entity, and therefore is separate from the marriage itself. The problem in some cases is that a judge can order you to liquidate assets owned by a trust, at least I've heard about such things happening.

The only thing I've ever heard of that is the closest thing to bullet proof is having an offshore trust. In April of 2022 I had Attorney Blake Harris on the podcast to talk about this. He specialized in offshore trusts through the Cook Islands. The reason this is bullet proof is that the Cook Islands are legally obligated by their own government to ignore court orders from the United States and other countries. So let's say that a judge orders a man to liquidate assets held by the offshore trust, they would comply with the court order by sending a request to the Cook Islands. The Cook Islands would simply ignore that order, and there isn't anything the court can do about it.

You can put everything you own into an offshore trust like that. You can even possibly negotiate with an employer to pay your salary to the trust. The trust would issue you a credit card that you can use to buy groceries, pay your bills, etc., but the money is never really yours. It belongs to the trust, and therefore cannot be taken from you in a divorce.

This setup sounds like the perfect solution, but if you're the average man who only makes $45,000 a year this is out of your price range. Managing a trust like this costs a pretty penny, and Blake Harris says that it's only really worth it if you have assets worth over a million dollars.

Now, like me when I rushed to get married at twenty years old, most men will read about this stuff and think they don't need protections like this because they don't have anything yet. That's not the point, she most likely isn't going to divorce you when you're young and penniless. She's going to wait ten to twenty years until you've built yourself up. She's going to wait until you've established yourself in a good career before she files for divorce. By that point, you WILL have money and assets worth fighting for. That's exactly what happened to me. Learn from my mistakes.

If I could go back and do things over, I wouldn't have gotten married so young. I would have spent my twenties spinning plates and building my fortune. I was running for that white picket fence though and got married at twenty years old. I wasn't even old enough to buy alcohol at my own wedding reception.

I was in the Navy at the time and both my Leading Chief Petty Officer and My Division Officer pulled me to the side and tried to talk me out of it. I was too pie-in-the-sky in-love to listen though. Don't get yourself into that kind of predicament, and certainly not at twenty years old.

What I tell my son is that he needs to wait until he's in his thirties before considering settling down and having a family. For men, we have our whole lives to do this. Women, unfortunately, don't. Women are racing a biological time clock where they will eventually run out of eggs. Men can safely have kids into their sixties if they want. I don't recommend waiting that long. I mean it's hard to keep up with a toddler when you're on a pacemaker. Just know that you have some time.

When it comes to children, I tell both my son and my daughter that there's really no great time to have kids. No matter what stage you are at financially, when you add a child to the mix, it becomes a financial burden. Not just with food and diapers, but with all the medical attention children tend to require. While there are no great times to have a child, some are better than others. Having a child in high school is the absolute worst anybody can do. It won't kill your dreams in life per se, but it will make attaining those dreams significantly harder than they need to be.

Waiting until you're in a committed, loving relationship is ideal for both men and women, but for women it's better for them to have children in their twenties when their bodies are designed for it. The later in life they wait, the harder the pregnancy is and the higher the chances for birth defects.

Waiting until you're at least in your thirties is ideal for men, because by then you'll most likely be established in your career and can better financially support a family at that time. Women don't necessarily have to wait until they're financially stable to support a family because they have men to help them and plenty of societal programs to help them raise that child.

Men in their thirties can easily pull and date girls in their twenties, so the timing couldn't be more perfect for both. Women tend to like older men anyway.

Once you've had the number of children you want, I personally recommend capping it off for good by getting a vasectomy. It fully protects you from accidentally getting your wife pregnant going forward, and if she does magically get pregnant, you know that she's been cheating on you, and it's time to cut her loose.

Having a vasectomy after you have kids will ensure that if things don't work out with the mother of your children, you won't accidentally get any other woman pregnant and potentially have to be on the hook for child support to multiple women.

If you plan to have children going forward, then I do not recommend getting a vasectomy. While there are procedures to reverse them, they aren't guaranteed. Make sure if you get one that you truly don't want any more children in the future.

The last thing I'll say about children is that if you found this book helpful in navigating your life, give this book to your son when he turns 18. I wish I knew all of this at 18, and if it helped you, it would certainly help him.

CONCLUSION

I've unpacked a lot since the Introduction.

I mentioned how writing books is difficult, and how anyone who says otherwise is either lying or a nerd. Now that I've made it to the end, I'm not sure if I will ever attempt to write another one. I suppose it all depends on how well this book is received and how well it's reviewed on Amazon.

I mentioned that I started writing this book when I was forty-two and would finish it when I was forty-three. I was off by a year. I'm now writing this conclusion at forty-four. That's what happens when you only dedicate every other Sunday to writing. Either way, I have a lot of respect for my colleagues in the space who regularly write and publish multiple books. I don't know how you guys knock those out. Hats off to you!

Another thing I mentioned in the introduction was how I was profoundly influenced early in life by my Karate Sensei, Fred Bode. He taught me the importance of mindset and told me to always strive to develop myself mentally, physically, and spiritually, all of which I cover in this book.

We covered the spiritual part in my Law of Attraction chapter although I purposely left out the spiritual explanation of The Law of Attraction to make it easier to understand. The truth is that the laws of the Universe are so precise that we are able to land a man on the moon and time the landing to within a fraction of a second. Learning to use the laws of the Universe in our lives can dramatically change outcomes for the better, and it doesn't really matter if you believe in some form of spirituality for it to work; it just does.

We covered the mental part in the education chapter, in the dating and spinning plates chapter, and the long-term relationship chapter. Its relevance in the education chapter is obvious: the idea behind education is to learn more which is developing yourself mentally. Don't automatically equate time spent in college with actually becoming educated though. College is a means to an end, and it is only required if the career you want to go into requires it. Otherwise, you can educate yourself for free, or at least much more cheaply, by reading books like this one. In the dating and relationship chapters, I discuss how we can develop ourselves mentally with regard to frame and being centered.

We covered the physical part in the diet and fitness chapter, and also a little bit in the dating and spinning plates chapter. It really is important for our overall health to stay fit and eat healthier. Many medical conditions can be avoided or cured by a solid foundation in fitness and health. In the dating and spinning plates chapter, we talked about how this affects our overall appearance and grooming. Being fit, healthy, and well-groomed also helps us tremendously when it comes to attracting the kind of women we want.

Mr. Bode never taught me about careers, making money, building wealth, or how to get the girls and keep them around longer. I had to learn that on my own, and I covered how to do it in the chapters on career, on how anyone can get rich, on dating and spinning plates, and finally in the long-term relationship chapters.

I've organized the book to make it follow a linear, ascending path of importance starting with The Law of Attraction and programming your subconscious mind to believe you can achieve whatever you want in life. This includes health, wealth, and love. The following chapters are tools to help you achieve those goals you set for yourself because The Law of Attraction is irrelevant and ineffective without the main ingredient: you taking action.

I really do wish I knew all of this at eighteen. If you are reading this and are over the age of thirty, you are probably thinking the same thing. Now you know these things though, so the question becomes, will you apply the knowledge? I hope the answer is yes. In either case, I certainly hope you consider giving this book to a young man coming out of high school. Perhaps a son, nephew, or little brother, so he can get the leg-up in life we never got because we were never taught   these things as young men. That way, forthcoming generations of young men will be able to say they *did* know all of this at 18, and, hopefully, they apply it and reap the benefits.

RECOMMENDED READING

Law of Attraction Material:
- The Practical Law of Attraction Course - **http://loa.comeonmanpod.com**
- Think and Grow Rich, by Napoleon Hill
- The Science Of Getting Rich, by Wallace D. Wattles
- Thought Vibration: The Law Of Attraction In The Thought World, by William Walter Atkinson
- The Last Law of Attraction Book You'll Ever Need To Read, by Andrew Kap

Financial Material:
- Total Money Makeover, by Dave Ramsey
- Money: Master The Game, by Tony Robbins
- Rich Dad Poor Dad, by Robert Kiyosaki
- Fake, by Robert Kiyosaki
- Bachelor Pad Economics, by Aaron Clarey

Dating, Relationship and Sexual Dynamics:
- How To Be A 3% Man, by Corey Wayne
- Atomic Attraction, by Christopher Canwell
- Dating Essentials for Men, by Dr. Robert Glover
- No More Mr. Nice Guy, by Dr. Robert Glover
- The Rational Male, by Rollo Tomassi
- The Players Handbook, by Rollo Tomassi
- A Dominant Masculine Presence, by RP Thor
- Praxeology: Volume 1 | Frame, by Rian Stone

ABOUT THE AUTHOR

Paul Bauer is a recovering 'Nice Guy' who, after a failed 14-year marriage and another unsuccessful 4.5-year relationship, finally realized that he was the common denominator in both situations. Determined to improve, he embarked on a journey to understand how he could elevate his interactions with women. Along the way, he discovered that enhancing one's skills in this area often leads to overall personal growth.

Paul now hosts the highly acclaimed podcast for men, "Come On Man," and has earned certification as a master life coach. Today, he extends his expertise to men worldwide, assisting them on their paths to self-improvement.

Visit **http://comeonmanpod.com**

Made in the USA
Columbia, SC
28 March 2025